D0011854

Spanish
verb handbook

Mike Zollo

Berlitz Publishing
New York   Munich   Singapore

Spanish Verb Handbook

Copyright © 2004 Mike Zollo

CONTACTING THE EDITORS
Every effort has been made to provide accurate information in this publication, but changes are inevitable. The publisher cannot be responsible for any resulting loss, inconvenience, or injury. We would appreciate it if readers would call our attention to any errors or outdated information by contacting Berlitz Publishing, 193 Morris Avenue, Springfield, NJ 07081, USA. Fax: 1-908-206-1103. email: comments@berlitzbooks.com

Published by Berlitz Publishing/Apa Publications GmbH & Co. Verlag KG, Singapore Branch, Singapore

Berlitz Trademark Reg. U.S. Patent Office and other countries. Marca Registrada.
Used under license from Berlitz Investment Corporation.

Cover Photo © Andy Stitt/Alamy; inset photo © PhotoAlto

Printed in Singapore by Insight Print Services (Pte) Ltd., December 2006

The Author:
Written by **Mike Zollo**, an experienced teacher, author and chief examiner. He is the chairman of the Association for Language Learning Spanish and Portuguese Committee.

The Series Editor:
Christopher Wightwick is a former UK representative on the Council of Europe Modern Languages Project and principal Inspector of Modern Languages for England.

Author's acknowledgment
I would like to thank Matilde Gutiérrez Manjón for her meticulous checking of the typescript and for some invaluable suggestions.

CONTENTS

How to Use This Handbook

This Handbook aims to provide a full description of the Spanish verb system for all learners and users of the Spanish language. It provides the following information:

• a chapter explaining the verb system in Spanish;

• the conjugation of fifty-eight verbs, grouped to show the common patterns underlying the system;

• a subject index to The Verb System in Spanish;

• a verb index, containing over twenty-two hundred verbs with their English meanings and references to the pattern(s) they follow.

An important feature of the book is that examples, showing many of the verbs in use, are given throughout The Verb System in Spanish and the Model Verbs.

THE VERB SYSTEM IN SPANISH

Use the Contents and Subject Index to find your way around this section, which describes the functions and forms of verbs in general. It provides information on the use of tenses, word order, the way verbs govern other parts of speech, and the way verbs are formed. It also describes methods of avoiding the passive, and it explains features such as the reflexive forms, the subjunctive, the verbs **ser** and **estar,** and the auxiliary verbs. It explains the main features of predictability and irregularity, and it illustrates key irregular verbs.

MODEL VERBS

Use the Verb Index to find your way around this section, which gives the full conjugation of one key model verb (**amar**) in all of its active and passive forms and of every tense of the other verbs in their active forms. This section provides models for all three groups of regular verbs plus the full range of spelling-change and stem-changing verbs, followed by all useful irregular verbs. This makes a total of fifty-eight model verbs.

The conjugation of each verb is given in all usable tenses. Tenses that have any irregularity are given in full. For tenses that are predictable, and most especially for compound tenses, only the first person singular form is given, as this is sufficient to enable you to predict the other forms within those tenses. Therefore, if a tense is not given in full, you can assume that it is regular.

For simple tenses, just look at the first model verb (**amar**) or at one of the three regular verb models (model verbs 2, 3, and 4) to figure out the endings needed. For compound tenses, check The Verb System in Spanish to decide which tense of which auxiliary verb is necessary, then look up the appropriate auxiliary verb (**haber, estar,** or **ser**) in the Model Verbs.

Where appropriate, the model verb pages also contain the following:

• A list of other verbs that follow the same pattern. If possible, all such verbs are given. If, however, they are too numerous to list, a selection of the most useful ones is given. There are, of course, verbs that stand alone, having no others following their model.

• Notes indicating the main features of this pattern and any variations or additional features affecting any of the verbs that basically follow that model.

• Short dialogues, narratives, or sentences that illustrate some of the different tenses and usages of these verbs.

For further information on how the verb system works, refer to The Verb System in Spanish.

SUBJECT INDEX

The Subject Index gives section references for all of the main grammatical terms used in The Verb System in Spanish.

VERB INDEX

For each of the twenty-two hundred or so verbs listed, the Verb Index gives information on whether it is transitive *(tr)*, intransitive *(intr)*, or reflexive *(refl)*, together with its English meaning. It also lists common secondary meanings and the main idiomatic expressions based on common verbs. Finally, each entry is referred to the model verb whose pattern it follows:

* **jugar (a)** (*intr*) play; gamble **21**

jugar el papel de (*intr*) act out, play a role

There are verbs that have more than one predictable or unpredictable variation from the norm. Such verbs have two numbers after them, and both model verb pages should be consulted in these cases.

HOW TO FIND THE INFORMATION YOU WANT

If you want to check on the form, meaning, or use of a verb, look it up in the Verb Index. This shows:

• which verbs are model verbs (indicated by an asterisk);

* abrir (*tr/intr*)   open, open up   **25**

• any preposition normally accompanying the verb;

echar la culpa a (*tr*)   blame   **2**

• whether the verb is transitive (*tr*), intransitive (*intr*), or reflexive (*refl*);

acabar (*tr*)   finish, complete   **2**

• the main English meaning of the verb, along with any important idiomatic uses;

entregar (*tr*)   deliver, hand over, hand in; turn over, yield   **7**

    entregarse a (*refl*)   become addicted

• a number indicating the model verb, which gives the conjugation of the verb, points out its irregularities, and lists verbs.

absorber (*tr*)   absorb   **3**

A
THE VERB SYSTEM IN SPANISH

What Verbs Do

Note: For more extensive treatment of the functions and uses of Spanish verbs, see the Berlitz *Spanish Grammar Handbook.*

1a Full Verbs

The great majority of verbs tell us about the action, state of mind, or (possibly changing) situation of the subject of the sentence. These are called *full* verbs.

Vivo **en una granja.**	*I live* on a farm.
Tenemos **un perro.**	*We have* a dog.

1b Auxiliary Verbs

A much smaller group of verbs is used almost exclusively to add something to the sense of a full verb—for example, to make a compound tense or to add a comment on an action. These are called *auxiliary* (helping) verbs.

He **comprado una casa.**	*I have* bought a house.
Suelo **ir a la oficina en coche.**	*I usually* go to the office by car.

1c Dual-Purpose Verbs

Some verbs can be used either with their full meanings or as auxiliaries. For example, the verb **estar** (to be)—used mostly to express the position, the state or the condition of something or somebody—is also used as the auxiliary verb to form the present progressive tense, which describes an action currently in progress.

Está **en la cocina.**	*She is* in the kitchen.
Está **preparando la cena.**	*She is* preparing dinner.

2 What Verbs Govern

A sentence can contain many items of information other than what is given by the subject and the main verb. Some of these items depend directly on the main verb and cannot be removed without leaving the sentence incomplete. These items are said to be *governed* by the verb.

2a Lone Verbs (Intransitive Verbs)

Some verbs do not normally govern an object [2c], though the sentence may, of course, contain adverbials that add to the meaning. These verbs are called *intransitive verbs* and are usually marked in verb lists and dictionaries as (intr).

Estaban charlando ruidosamente.	*They were chatting noisily.*

They were chatting makes sense by itself. Although we know how they were chatting (noisily), this information is not necessary for the sentence to make sense.

2b Verbs Linking Equals: The Complement

A small number of verbs simply act as links between the subject and another word or phrase, which is called the *complement* of the verb. Usually the complement is a noun phrase, referring to the same person or thing as the subject.

Mi padre fue *profesor*.	My father was *a teacher*.

It can be seen that the noun phrase complement (*a teacher*) refers to the subject (*my father*).

2c Verbs with One Object (Transitive Verbs)

Many verbs take a *direct object* (i.e., the person or thing affected by the main verb). These verbs are *transitive*. They are usually marked in dictionaries and verb lists as (tr). A direct object answers the question *what?* or *whom?* Intransitive verbs cannot have a direct object.

Mi amigo compró *un perro*.	My friend bought *a dog*.

Here, *a dog* is what my friend bought, so it is the direct object of *bought*.

2d   Verbs That Can Be Both Transitive and Intransitive

Many verbs can be used both transitively and intransitively in Spanish, either standing alone or having an object. They may be listed as (tr/intr) in verb lists and dictionaries.

Mis amigos *hablaban* mucho.	My friends *were talking* a lot.
***Ellos hablaban español*.**	*They were speaking Spanish.*

2e   Verbs with Two Objects: Direct and Indirect

Some transitive verbs describe the transfer of the direct object to another person (or possibly thing). This person is then the *indirect object* of the verb. With some verbs the idea can be extended to include people indirectly affected by the action of the verb. The indirect object answers the question *to whom?* or *for whom?*

Siempre le da *diez pesos al mendigo*.	He always gives *ten pesos to the beggar*.

The money is the direct object, and the beggar—the beneficiary — is the indirect object.

2f   Objects That Refer to the Subject: Reflexive Verbs

Another type of verb describes an action that 'rebounds' or 'reflects' on the subject; in other words, the subject and the indirect object are one and the same. In English, they will often involve the use of one of the '-self' pronouns. These are called *reflexive verbs*; the vast majority of these verbs can be used as ordinary transitive verbs too—e.g., **lavar** (to wash), **lavarse** (wash oneself). Many verbs are reflexive in Spanish but not in English.

Se está duchando.	*He's taking a shower.*
Todos los días, se despertaba temprano.	*Every day, he used to wake up early.*
Se lavó las manos antes de comer.	*He washed his hands before eating.*

2g Verbs Plus Prepositions

Many verbs, including those describing motion or situation, are supported by an adverb or a prepositional phrase.

Estamos aquí.	We are *here.*
Vive en aquella casa.	He lives *in that house.*

2h Verbs Governing Verbs

(i) Verbs + infinitives

This is a very common structure in Spanish. It has many expressions based on a modal auxiliary verb [3 below].

Queremos salir a las ocho.	*We want to go out at eight.*
Me gusta mucho bailar.	*I like dancing very much.*
¿Sabes nadar?	*Do you know how to swim?*

(ii) Verbs + prepositions + infinitives

Spanish also has a number of these structures. They are very similar to the one above, but with a preposition between the auxiliary verb and the main verb.

Vamos a cenar en un restaurante.	*We are going to dine in a restaurant.*

Acababan de llegar.	*They had just arrived.*
Salió sin cerrar **la puerta.**	*She went out without shutting the door.*

(iii)   Verbs + participles

(A) Verb + present participle: Like English, Spanish has a way of describing an action in progress. This is done by using the verb **estar** (be) with the present participle of a verb, usually referred to by Spanish teachers as the *gerund*.

Estábamos comiendo **cuando llegó.**	*We were eating* when he arrived.

(B) Verb + past participle: Past events can be described by using the auxiliary verb **haber** with the past participle of a verb. In addition, **ser** plus the past participle of a verb is used to form the passive [▷ 9], and **estar** plus the past participle of a verb can be used to describe a state resulting from an action.

El capitán *ha llegado.*	The captain *has arrived.*
La nueva guía *será publicada* **en mayo.**	The new guide *will be published* in May.
La ventana *está rota.*	The window *is broken.*

2i   Position of Verbs in the Sentence

(i)   Generally speaking, the word order in a sentence in Spanish is similar to that of a sentence in English; if anything, word order in Spanish is slightly more flexible, but experience is more useful here than any hard-and-fast rules.

(ii)   One important difference is that verbs in Spanish are usually found without an accompanying subject pronoun [▷ 10a]. This is because each verb ending is clear and distinct, not only in the written, but also in the spoken form. The verb endings themselves, therefore, convey the idea of person without the need for subject pronouns. However, the pronouns are used for emphasis, contrast, or clarity, when necessary.

—¿Quién rompió la ventana?	"Who broke the window?"
—¡La rompió *él*, señor!	"*He* broke it, sir!"
—Bueno, *yo* voy al teatro y	So, *I*'m going to the theater, and
tú vas al cine, ¿no es así?	*you*'re going to the movies, right?
—¿Tiene *usted* coche?	Do *you* have a car?

(iii) Questions

Questions in English are usually formed by inverting verb and subject (with or without the auxiliary *do*). However, in Spanish such inversion is both not very common and impossible to make unless there is a separate subject pronoun. Instead, questions are indicated by adding the inverted question mark at the beginning of the sentence in written Spanish, and by the question intonation pattern in spoken Spanish.

Mi madre tiene un coche nuevo.	My mother has a new car.
¿Tu madre tiene un coche nuevo? ⎫	
¿Tiene tu madre un coche nuevo? ⎭	Does your mother have a new car?
Tienes muchos amigos.	You have a lot of friends.
¿Tienes muchos amigos?	Do you have many friends?

(iv) Negative expressions

Negative expressions in Spanish are quite straightforward and do not affect the position of the verb in the sentence. *No* and *not* are both translated by **no,** which is placed immediately before the verb and any dependent object pronouns.

Mi novio *no* va a la playa conmigo.	My boyfriend is *not* going to the beach with me.
—¿Lo tienes tú?	"Do you have it?"
—No, *no* lo tengo.	"No, I do*n't* have it."
—¿Has recibido la carta?	"Have you received the letter?"
—No, *no* la he recibido.	"No, I have*n't* received it."

No can be combined with other negative expressions (**nada, nunca, nadie,** etc.), which are usually placed around the verb.

No le dije *nada.*	I said *nothing* to him.
No fuimos *nunca* a Bogotá.	We *never* went to Bogota.

7

THE VERB SYSTEM IN SPANISH

No conocí a *nadie* en
Las Vegas.

I did*n't* meet *anyone*
in Las Vegas.

Note: **Nadie** (and sometimes **nada** and **nunca**) can begin a sentence, in which case there is no need for **no**. This does not affect the position of the verb in the sentence.

Nadie llama a la puerta.
Nada se pudo recuperar.
Nunca fuimos a Bogotá.

There is *nobody* knocking at the door.
Nothing could be recovered.
We *never* went to Bogota.

3 | Attitudes to Action: Modal Verbs

3a The Function of Modal Verbs

Modal auxiliary verbs, as mentioned in 2h(i) above, modify full verbs to express additional viewpoints such as possibility, desire, and obligation. They are used in the appropriate persons and tenses, followed by the infinitives of the full verbs.

3b The Verbs and Their Meanings

The following are the main modal auxiliary verbs used in Spanish:

(i) *poder* be able to, can

No *puedo* ir contigo.	*I ca*n't go with you.

(ii) *querer* want to, wish to

El testigo no *quería* decir más.	The witness *did*n't *want to* say anything else.

(iii) *gustar* please

This verb is used to express the idea of *liking.*

No *le gustaba* bailar.	He *did*n't *like* to dance.
¿*Te gustaría* salir conmigo?	*Would you like* to go out with me?

(iv) *deber* have to, must, be obliged to, ought to, should

¡No *debes* hacer eso!	*You must* not do that!
Deberían escuchar al profesor.	*They should/ought to* listen to the teacher.

(v) ***deber de*** *must*

> This verb is used to express probability.

Debe de estar ya en Buenos Aires.	*He must* be in Buenos Aires by now.

(vi) ***tener que*** *have to, must, be obliged to*

Tenemos que ir a casa.	*We have to* go home.

(vii) ***dejar*** *allow, permit*

Mis padres no me dejarán salir.	My parents *will* not *let* me go out.

(viii) ***permitir*** *permit, allow*

No se permite estacionar aquí.	Parking *is* not *allowed* here.

(ix) ***hacer*** *get something done, do, make*

Voy a hacer reparar mi coche.	I'm going to *get* my car fixed / repaired.

Note: **Gustar** and other verbs like it, such as **apetecer**, are known as impersonal or 'back-to-front' verbs. For more details on their use, see Berlitz *Spanish Grammar Handbook*.

Verb Forms Not Related to Time

Verbs are very versatile words, A verb form alone will usually tell you *who, what,* and *when* about the action/idea of the verb: *who* is responsible for it, *what* the action/idea is, *when* it takes place. However, there are some verb forms that do not specify the *who* or *when*.

4a   The Infinitive

The key form of the verb, as found in a verb list or dictionary — and in the Verb Index of this book — is the *infinitive*, and this only explains *what* is being described. In Spanish, the infinitive form of all verbs ends in one of the following: **-ar, -er, -ir** (for example, am**ar**, com**er**, viv**ir**).

4b   The Two Participles

(i)   *The present participle*

This is a form of the verb often used to describe an action in progress; in Spanish, it is usually known as the *gerund.* The Spanish gerund form consists of the basic verb stem and the ending **-ando** (**-ar** verbs) or **-iendo** (**-er** and **-ir** verbs). Its most common use is with the auxiliary verb **estar,** to form the progressive tenses [6a(ii) and 6b(ii)]; but it can also be used by itself, provided that its subject and the subject of the other verb in the sentence are the same.

La chica está *dibujando* un gato.	The girl is *drawing* a cat.
Estaban *jugando* fútbol cuando los vi.	They were *playing* soccer when I saw them.
***Cruzando* la calle, vi un coche antiguo.**	*Crossing* the street, I saw an old car.

Note: Although the present participle is often referred to as the *gerund* in Spanish, it is important not to confuse this term with the English gerund (the form that ends in '-ing'). The English gerund is often used in situations where Spanish uses an infinitive.

11

THE VERB SYSTEM IN SPANISH

Me gusta *bailar*.	I like *dancing*.
Prohibido *fumar*.	No *smoking*.

(ii)   *The past participle*

This form is used to describe an action that is finished. In Spanish, it ends in **-ado** (**-ar** verbs) or **-ido** (**-er** and **-ir** verbs). [6b(iv) for irregular past participles.] It is very often used with the auxiliary verb **haber** to form the perfect tenses and other compound tenses, but it is also used in other ways, including as an adjective and to form the passive. When used with **haber** in compound tenses, it does *not* need to agree with either the object or the subject, but elsewhere it does.

Ha *salido* **sin decir nada.**	He has *gone out* without saying anything.
Estos son los cuadros *pintados* **por Picasso.**	These are the pictures *painted* by Picasso.
En la calle había unas revistas quemadas.	In the street there were some *burnt* magazines.
Esta casa fue *construida* **por mi padre.**	This house was *built* by my father.

Note: The past participle is used as part of a compound tense in the first example above, as an adjective in the second and the third, and as part of a passive construction in the fourth.

In these last three examples, therefore, the past participles agree with the noun to which they relate, as it happens when the past participle is used as an adjective or is used to form the passive.

5 | The Passage of Time and the Use of Tenses

5a What Do Tenses Tell Us?

Tenses are grammatical structures that often reflect a way of looking at an event as well as just recording when it takes place. Both the number of tenses and the denominations given to them vary from one language to another, though fortunately the main Spanish tenses correspond closely to those in English.

5b One Word or Two? Simple and Compound Tenses

Most verb forms consist of two parts. One describes *what* is going on; this basic part is called the *stem* or *root* of the verb, and for most tenses in Spanish it is the infinitive minus the **-ar, -er,** or **-ir** (for example, for the verbs **amar, comer,** and **vivir** these stems are **am-, com-,** and **viv-**). The other part defines *who* is responsible and *when* it is happening. There are two sorts of tenses: simple tenses and compound tenses.

(i) Simple tenses

These tenses are formed by adding special sets of endings to a basic stem or root: the stem tells *what* the action or idea is, and the ending gives the *who* and *when* information.

(ii) Compound tenses

These tenses use an auxiliary (helping) verb along with a special form of the main verb—a participle or the infinitive itself.

Thus, in the language of grammar, a simple tense is a one-word form, while a compound tense uses two or more words. Not counting the passive, in which all tenses are compound, Spanish has five simple tenses (seven including the subjunctive) and seven compound tenses (nine including the subjunctive). This is not as daunting as it seems, because some tenses are not used very often, especially in speech, and so it will probably be enough simply to be able to recognize them when you hear or read Spanish. In any case, once you know how to use the auxiliary verbs **haber, ser,** and **estar,** any compound tense can be formed by adding the appropriate participle.

THE VERB SYSTEM IN SPANISH

Note: In Spanish, the verb endings are clear and distinctive in both written and spoken language, and so subject pronouns (the person words listed in 10a below) are not usually needed, since the verb endings themselves make it *clear* who is involved [▷ 2i(ii)].

5c Auxiliary Verbs Used to Form Compound Tenses

In Spanish, the compound tenses fall into two groups, each using a different auxiliary verb. They should both prove easy for English speakers to master, as the positive forms are composed in exactly the same way as their equivalents in English.

(i) The progressive tenses

These tenses are used to describe actions that are in progress at the time being referred to. In English, they are easily identified, as they are formed by the appropriate form of the verb *be* followed by the main verb in the '-ing' form. Spanish uses an identical structure: the appropriate form of the verb **estar** followed by the *gerund* [▷ 4b(i)]. The two main tenses of this type are the present progressive and imperfect progressive: both describe an action in a more graphic, vivid way than their present and imperfect tense counterparts [▷ 6a(ii) and 6b(ii) below]. Note that Spanish uses the progressive tenses less than English, often preferring to use a simple tense.

¿**No lo oyes?** *Están llamando* knocking **a la puerta.**	Can't you hear? *They are* at the door.
Cuando me llamaste, *estaba planchando* **una camisa.**	When you called me *I was ironing* a shirt.

(ii) The compound past tenses

In English, these tenses are formed with the appropriate form of the verb *have*. Again, Spanish uses an identical structure: the appropriate form of the verb **haber** followed by the past participle.

Note: This is the only use of **haber** apart from the forms **hay, había,** etc., meaning *there is/are, there was/were*, etc. The verb **tener** is the verb normally used to convey the idea of possession.

¡*Ha llegado* **Manuel!**	Manuel *has arrived!*
Habían visto a Mariluz en la discoteca.	*They had seen* Mariluz at the disco.

Note: The past participle is also used to form all passive forms [▷ 9 below].

6 | Statements of Probable Fact: The Indicative

Verb forms and tenses that make a positive statement are said to be *indicative*. [Contrast this with the subjunctive: ➤ 8.]

In all verbs there are some tenses whose stems and endings can be predicted if you know one of the other parts of the verb. Parts that cannot be predicted in this way have to be learned, but once the principal parts are known, it is usually possible to predict other parts. It is helpful to know how to obtain the stem, to which the endings for each tense are added, and any spelling adjustments that may need to be made. The following sections give a breakdown of the main uses of each tense, and explain how to get the stem and endings for each tense, along with any pitfalls to watch out for.

6a   *The Present Tense*

In Spanish, the present tense can be used to convey the following ideas:

• What the situation is *now*.

En este momento mi amigo *habla* con el profesor de inglés.	At this moment my friend *is talking* to the English teacher.

• What happens *sometimes* or *usually*.

En casa, sólo *hablamos* español.	At home, *we* only *speak* Spanish.

• What is going to happen *(quite) soon*.

Mañana me *voy* a Caracas.	Tomorrow *I'm going* to Caracas.

• What has been happening *up to now* and may continue to happen.

15

THE VERB SYSTEM IN SPANISH

| Llevamos diez minutos esperando. | We've been waiting for ten minutes. |
| Estudio español desde hace cuatro años. | I've been studying Spanish for four years. |

(i)   The present indicative

This tense is formed by adding a set of endings to the stem of the verb, which consists of the infinitive with the **-ar, -er,** or **-ir** ending removed.

comprar (buy)	*comer* (eat)	*vivir* (live)
compr**o**	com**o**	viv**o**
compr**as**	com**es**	viv**es**
compr**a**	com**e**	viv**e**
compr**amos**	com**emos**	viv**imos**
compr**áis**	com**éis**	viv**ís**
compr**an**	com**en**	viv**en**

Be careful with all of the following [10b]:

• Spelling-change verbs with changes to the final consonant of their stem   10b(ii).
• Stem-changing verbs (all groups)   10b(v).
• Verbs whose first person singular stem ends in **-g-** (**poner,** etc.)   10b(vi).
• Verbs whose first person singular stem ends in **-zc-** (verbs ending in **-ocer, -ecer, -ucir**)   10b(vii).
• Verbs ending in **-uir** (**concluir,** etc.)   10b(iii).
• Verbs whose first person singular ending is **-oy** (**dar, estar, ir, ser**)   10b(viii).

For other irregular verbs, see Model Verbs.

(ii)   The present progressive

This is formed by using the present tense of **estar** plus the *gerund* of the verb [4b(i)].

comprar → **comprando**   comer → **comiendo**   vivir → **viviendo**

Note: The following irregularities occur in the *gerund*:

• If the **-i-** of the ending comes between vowels, it becomes **-y: leer** (*read*) → **leyendo,** **oír** (*hear*) → **oyendo,** and others [Model Verbs 12,13].
• After **-ll-** and **-ñ-** the **-i-** is dropped: **zambullir** (*dive*) → **zambullendo, gruñir** (*grunt*) → **gruñendo.**
• The stressed vowel of the stem of some stem-changing verbs changes: **dormir** (*sleep*) → **durmiendo, vestir** (*dress*) → **vistiendo,** etc.

6b *The Past Tenses*

(i) *The imperfect indicative*

This tense is used for:
• repeated or habitual actions in the past;
• descriptions of things or people in the past;
• ongoing actions in the past, often as settings or backgrounds to other actions.

Iba **a La Habana todos los años.**	*He used to go* to Havana every year.
Era **una casa muy grande.**	*It was* a very big house.
Escribía **una carta cuando entré.**	*He was writing* a letter when I came in.

The imperfect indicative is formed by removing the infinitive ending and adding endings as follows:

comprar	*comer*	*vivir*
compr**aba**	com**ía**	viv**ía**
compr**abas**	com**ías**	viv**ías**
compr**aba**	com**ía**	viv**ía**
compr**ábamos**	com**íamos**	viv**íamos**
compr**abais**	com**íais**	viv**íais**
compr**aban**	com**ían**	viv**ían**

Note: The following verbs are irregular in the imperfect:

ser (be)	*ir* (go)
era	**iba**
eras	**ibas**
era	**iba**
éramos	**íbamos**
erais	**ibais**
eran	**iban**

Ver (*see*) retains the **-e-**: **veía**, etc.

(ii) *The imperfect progressive*

This tense is often used when a more vivid description of an ongoing action is needed. It is formed by using the appropriate imperfect tense form of **estar** followed by the *gerund* [▷ 5c(i) and compare ▷ 6a(ii)].

THE VERB SYSTEM IN SPANISH

> **Cuando llegaste, *yo estaba durmiendo*.**
>
> When you arrived, *I was sleeping.*

(iii) *The preterite*

This tense is used for a single, completed action in the past, even if it spanned a long period, as long as the precise amount of time is defined.

> ***Compraron* este terreno el año pasado.**
>
> *They bought* this land last year.
>
> ***Vivió* unos veinte años en Caracas.**
>
> *She lived* for about twenty years in Caracas.

The preterite is formed by removing the infinitive ending and adding the endings shown below. Note the stressed endings in the first and third persons singular.

comprar	*comer*	*vivir*
compr**é**	com**í**	viv**í**
compr**aste**	com**iste**	viv**iste**
compr**ó**	com**ió**	viv**ió**
compr**amos**	com**imos**	viv**imos**
compr**asteis**	com**isteis**	viv**isteis**
compr**aron**	com**ieron**	viv**ieron**

Note: Watch out for the **pretérito grave** [10b(ix)], where the ending of the first and third persons singular is not stressed and the stem can be irregular. Verbs of this type are marked *(pg)* in the Model Verbs. They include some very common verbs (**querer, tener, decir, poder,** etc.).

tener (have)	*decir (say)*
tuve	dije
tuviste	dijiste
tuvo	dijo
tuvimos	dijimos
tuvisteis	dijisteis
tuvieron	dijeron

There are further irregularities in the following types of verb, which should be checked in the relevant paragraph or section:
- Stem-changing verbs [10b(v)], types 2 and 3.
- Spelling-change verbs [10b(ii)].
- **Dar, ir, ser** [Model Verbs].

18

• Verbs where the third person plural ending (**-ieron**) follows a vowel, **-ll-**, or **-ñ-** [Model Verbs].

(iv)   The rest of the past tenses in Spanish are compound tenses. They are formed using the appropriate tense of the auxiliary verb **haber** [Model Verbs] and the past participle [4b (ii) and 6b(v)]. Note the following irregular past participles:

abrir (open)	**abierto**
cubrir (cover)	**cubierto**
descubrir (discover, uncover)	**descubierto**
decir (say, tell)	**dicho**
disolver (dissolve)	**disuelto**
escribir (write)	**escrito**
freír (fry)	**frito**
hacer (make, do)	**hecho**
poner (put)	**puesto**
resolver (solve, resolve)	**resuelto**
romper (break)	**roto**
ver (see)	**visto**
volver (turn, return)	**vuelto**

Note: Compounds of these verbs have past participles with the same irregularities.

(v)   The past participle is used with the appropriate tense of the auxiliary verb **haber** to form the following compound tenses, which largely correspond to their English equivalents.

(A) Present perfect tense (present of **haber** + past participle) The present perfect tense is usually used to refer to an action that has recently taken place, much as in English, though the preterite tense can be used in much the same way.

Hemos terminado el trabajo.	*We have finished* the work.

(B) Pluperfect tense (imperfect of **haber** + past participle) The pluperfect tense is used to take an extra step back from a time already in the past, which is the focus of attention. It corresponds to the English *had* + past participle.

Lo ***habían visto*** antes.	*They had seen* him before.

(C) Past anterior tense (preterite of **haber** + past participle)
The past anterior tense has the same meaning as the pluperfect, i.e., describing an action that *had taken place when*. . . . It
is used instead of the pluperfect after certain expressions and
is fairly rare. See the Berlitz *Spanish Grammar Handbook* for
further explanation.

Antes de que *hube salido,* llegó a casa.	Before *I went out*, he arrived home.

(D) Future perfect tense (future of **haber** + past participle)
The future perfect tense is used to take a step forward from a
time in the past to express the idea of *will have* + past participle.

***Habrá comido* ya, y no querrá nada más.**	*He will* already *have eaten* and won't want anything else.

(E) Conditional perfect tense (conditional of **haber** + past
participle)
The conditional perfect tense is used to convey the idea of
would have. . . , and is often used to express something hypothetical or unfulfilled.

***Habríamos tomado el sol,* pero llovía.**	*We would have sunbathed*, but it was raining.

6c   The Future Tense

In Spanish, the future can be conveyed in one of two ways:
the *future immediate* and the *future simple*.

(i)   The future immediate

This describes an action about to happen. It is formed by the
appropriate form of the verb **ir** plus **a** plus the infinitive of the
verb. The structure is very similar to its equivalent in English.

***Vamos a nadar* en el mar.**	*We are going to swim* in the sea.
El jefe *va a volver* mañana.	The boss *is going to return* tomorrow.

(ii) *The future simple*

This is used for the following:

• Actions that are expected to happen in the future.

La semana que viene, *iremos* a Valparaíso.	Next week *we'll go* to Valparaiso.

• To express instructions.

Después de comer, *lavarás* los platos, ¿no?	After eating, *you'll wash* the dishes, won't you?

• To express predictions.

***Lloverá* esta tarde.**	*It will rain* this afternoon.

• To express probability.

***Tendrá* unos sesenta años.**	*He's probably* about sixty.

The future simple is formed by adding the appropriate set of endings to the *whole of the infinitive*. The only possible irregularity is in the stem, which always ends in **-r-** (see the irregular stems below). The endings are the same for all verbs. Note the stress accent on all the endings except **-emos.**

comprar	*comer*	*vivir*
comprar**é**	comer**é**	vivir**é**
comprar**ás**	comer**ás**	vivir**ás**
comprar**á**	comer**á**	vivir**á**
comprar**emos**	comer**emos**	vivir**emos**
comprar**éis**	comer**éis**	vivir**éis**
comprar**án**	comer**án**	vivir**án**

Note: The stems of the following verbs are irregular:

caber (fit)	**cabré**
decir (say)	**diré**
haber (have)	**habré**
hacer (do, make)	**haré**
poder (be able)	**podré**
poner (put)	**pondré**

querer (want, love)	**querré**
saber (know)	**sabré**
tener (have)	**tendré**
valer (be worth)	**valdré**
venir (come)	**vendré**

The compounds of any of these verbs have the same irregularities [▶ 10c].

6d   The (Present) Conditional: What If?

Commonly referred to as 'the conditional,' the present conditional tense is used—broadly speaking—as the equivalent of *would* or *should* in English (but not necessarily with the sense of obligation). In the actual expression of conditions, it is used to indicate the outcome rather than the condition itself. It can also be used to express probability and the future in the past.

Me gustaría comprarlos.	*I'd like to buy them.*
Si tuviera dinero, *viviría* en San Francisco.	If he had the money, *he'd live* in San Francisco.
***Tendría* unos diez años cuando la vi por última vez.**	*She would have been* about ten the last time I saw her.
Dijo que después de llegar, *llamaría* a su madre.	He said that after arriving *he would call* his mother.

The (present) conditional has the same stem as the future tense [▶ 6c]. The endings are the same as the **-er/-ir** imperfect endings [▶ 6b(i)].

comprar	*comer*	*vivir*
compra**ría**	come**ría**	vivi**ría**
compra**rías**	come**rías**	vivi**rías**
compra**ría**	come**ría**	vivi**ría**
compra**ríamos**	come**ríamos**	vivi**ríamos**
compra**ríais**	come**ríais**	vivi**ríais**
compra**rían**	come**rían**	vivi**rían**

Note: The irregular stems in 6c also apply to the (present) conditional.

7 Requests and Commands: The Imperative

Orders and instructions can be given in a variety of ways:

• Expressing obligations.

Tienes que **limpiar tu cuarto.**	*You have to* clean your room.

• Using the infinitive.

Lavar **bien la fruta antes de comerla.**	*Wash* fruit well before eating it.

• Using the imperative forms of the verb, as detailed below.

7a   The Informal Imperative Positive Singular

The informal imperative positive singular (the **tú** form) is formed by removing the final **-s** from the second person singular form of the present indicative tense.

compras → **compra**   comes → **come**   vives → **vive**

Note: The following verbs have irregular imperative forms:

decir	**di**	salir	**sal**
hacer	**haz**	ser	**sé**
ir	**ve**	tener	**ten**
poner	**pon**	venir	**ven**

¡*Compra* **el mejor vino de España!**	*Buy* the best wine of Spain!
¡*Sal* **de ahí en seguida!**	*Get out* of there at once!

Note also that pronouns can be attached to the end of positive imperatives. In that case, a written accent may be necessary to maintain the correct stress.

Dímelo.	Tell it to me.

7b   The Informal Imperative Positive Plural

The informal imperative positive plural (the **vosotros** form) is formed by removing the **-r** of the infinitive and adding **-d**. This is one of three instances where the endings of **-er** and **-ir** verbs differ—the first and second person plural of the present indicative being the other two [10b(i)]. Note that the **-d** drops out when the reflexive pronoun **-os** is added.

comprar	compra**d**	lavar(se)	lava**os**
comer	come**d**	poner(se)	pone**os**
vivir	vivi**d**	divertir(se)	divert**íos**

Note: • An accent is added on **-í-** when **-os** is added.

• The informal imperative positive plural for **irse** is **idos** (go away).

• The **vosotros** form is considered informal in Spain, but in most Latin American countries it is considered rather formal and is used in a limited manner. The alternative second person plural form, **ustedes,** is widely used for both formal and informal situations in the Latin American region.

Comed y **bebed** todo.	*Eat* and *drink* it all.
Ponedlos en la mesa.	*Put them* on the table.
Sentaos, chicos.	*Sit down,* boys.

7c   Negative Informal Imperatives and All Formal Imperatives

The negative informal (**tú** and **vosotros**) and the positive formal (**usted** and **ustedes**) imperatives are formed in the same way as—or are the same as—their corresponding present subjunctive forms. Note that in the negative imperatives the object pronouns come immediately before the verb.

Informal negative

no compr**es**	no com**as**	no viv**as**
no compr**éis**	no com**áis**	no viv**áis**
no te lav**es**	no te pon**gas**	no te diviert**as**
no os lav**éis**	no os pon**gáis**	no os divirt**áis**

Formal positive

compr**e**	com**a**	viv**a**
compr**en**	com**an**	viv**an**

Formal negative

no compr**e**	no com**a**	no viv**a**
no compr**en**	no com**an**	no viv**an**
no se lav**e**	no se pon**ga**	no se divier**ta**
no se lav**en**	no se pon**gan**	no se divier**tan**

Any irregularity in the present subjunctive tense will, of course, occur in these imperatives as well [8].

Vuelvan **mañana.**	*Come back* tomorrow.
Póngase **este sombrero.**	*Put* this hat *on.*
Llévenlos **a casa.**	*Take them* home.
¡No *te caigas*!	Don't *fall!*
No las *comáis.*	Don't *eat* them.
¡No me *miren* así!	Don't *look at* me like that!
No *se sienten* allí.	Don't *sit* there.
No las *compre.*	Don't *buy* them.

7d   *Summary of Imperative Forms*

	Informal		Formal
Positive singular	compra	singular	compre
(tú)	come	**(usted)**	coma
	vive		viva
plural	comprad	plural	compren
(vosotros)	comed	**(ustedes)**	coman
	vivid		vivan
Negative singular	no compres	singular	no compre
(tú)	no comas	**(usted)**	no coma
	no vivas		no viva
plural	no compréis	plural	no compren
(vosotros)	no comáis	**(ustedes)**	no coman
	no viváis		no vivan

Areas of Uncertainty: The Subjunctive

The subjunctive is used whenever a less-than-fact statement is made; it can be a case of doubt or uncertainty, or a case of unfulfilled or hypothetical action. For more detailed explanation, see the Berlitz *Spanish Grammar Handbook*.

8a   *The Present Subjunctive*

Stem: Remove ending from the first person singular form of the present indicative tense.
Endings: Invert the order given for the indicative endings, i.e., for **-ar** verbs use the endings that begin with **-e-**, and for **-er** and **-ir** verbs use the endings that begin with **-a-**.

comprar	*comer*	*vivir*
compr**e**	com**a**	viv**a**
compr**es**	com**as**	viv**as**
compr**e**	com**a**	viv**a**
compr**emos**	com**amos**	viv**amos**
compr**éis**	com**áis**	viv**áis**
compr**en**	com**an**	viv**an**

Note: Watch out for the following:

• Stem-changing verbs of all types [10b(v)]. Pay particular attention to the further **e → i** and **o → u** changes in the second and third persons plural forms, types 2 and 3.
• Spelling changes in the final consonant of the stem [10b(ii)].
• Stems ending in **-g-** (**poner**, etc.) [10b(vi)].
• Stems with **-zc-** (verbs ending in **-ocer, -ecer, -ucir**) [10b(vii)].
• Verbs ending in **-uir** (**concluir**, etc.) [10b(iii)].

• Irregular present subjunctives: **caber → quepa, haber → haya, ir → vaya, saber → sepa, ser → sea**. (For full sets of forms, see the Model Verbs.)

No quiero que *comas* eso.	I don't want you to *eat* that.
Cuando *lleguemos*, tomaremos un café.	We'll have a coffee when *we arrive.*

8b   The Imperfect Subjunctive

Stem: Remove the ending from the third person plural form of the preterite tense.
Endings: There are two forms of this tense, which are totally interchangeable except that the **-ra** forms alone can be used to replace the conditional. (See the Berlitz *Spanish Grammar Handbook* for detailed explanation.)

-ra forms

comprara	comiera	viviera
compraras	comieras	vivieras
comprara	comiera	viviera
compráramos	comiéramos	viviéramos
comprarais	comierais	vivierais
compraran	comieran	vivieran

-se forms

comprase	comiese	viviese
comprases	comieses	vivieses
comprase	comiese	viviese
comprásemos	comiésemos	viviésemos
compraseis	comieseis	vivieseis
comprasen	comiesen	viviesen

Any of the stem irregularities that occur in the preterite tense [6b(iii)] are carried right through both forms of the imperfect subjunctive.

mentir (lie)	**mintieron**	**mintiera/mintiese**
dormir (sleep)	**durmieron**	**durmiera/durmiese**
leer (read)	**leyeron**	**leyera/leyese**
decir (say)	**dijeron**	**dijera/dijese**
ir/ser (go/be)	**fueron**	**fuera/fuese**

Si *fuera* rico, me compraría un Ferrari.	If *I were* rich, I'd buy a Ferrari.
Les dijo que *se callasen*.	He told them to *shut up*.

8c   Compound Subjunctive Tenses

The compound subjunctive tenses are formed by using the appropriate subjunctive tense of the auxiliary verb **haber** followed by the past participle of the main verb, as can be seen clearly in the Model Verbs [6b(iv) and 6b(v)].

9 | Things Done to You: The Passive

9a The True Passive

Used to express an action from the point of view of the person or thing undergoing the action, the true passive is formed in Spanish in the same way as in English: use the appropriate form of the verb **ser** (be) followed by the past participle of the verb. (See Model Verbs for the complete conjugation of **ser**.) The only other thing to remember is that the past participle has to agree in gender and number with the subject, as in the following examples.

La ventana *fue rota* por ese chico.	The window *was broken* by that boy.
Ramón *fue atropellado* por un camión.	Ramón *was run over* by a truck / lorry.
Mis hermanas *han sido contratadas* por una compañía grande.	My sisters *have been hired* by a big company.

9b Alternatives to the True Passive

There are several ways of avoiding the true passive:

• Use the third person plural form of the verb impersonally.

***Me dijeron* que va a llover.**	*I was told (they told me)* that it is going to rain.
***Los robaron* ayer.**	*They were stolen (someone stole them)* yesterday.

• Invert the sentence if there is an agent that you can turn into the subject.

Lo mataron *los moros*.	He was killed by *the Moors* (*the Moors* killed him).

• Make the verb reflexive (this can only be done when the subject is inanimate).

La puerta *se cerró*.	The door *was closed* (*literally*: The door *closed itself*).
***Se cultiva* el arroz en la región de Valencia.**	Rice *is grown* (*literally: grows itself*) in the Valencia region.

• Use the redundant object pronoun.

La blusa *la* compró mi madre.	The blouse was bought by my mother (*literally*: The blouse — my mother bought *it*).

10 Types of Verb in Spanish

10a Predictability

The whole set of a verb's forms, including all tense forms, is known as its *conjugation*. Within each tense in Spanish, there are six different forms of the verb, each one corresponding to a particular person as follows:

first person singular:	**yo**	I
second person singular:	**tú**	you (familiar)
	usted	you (formal)
third person singular:	**él**	he
	ella	she
first person plural:	**nosotros/as**	we
second person plural:	**vosotros/as**	you (familiar plural)
	ustedes	you (formal plural)
third person plural:	**ellos**	they (masculine)
	ellas	they (feminine)

Note: *He, she*, and *you* (formal singular) share the same verb forms: *they* and *you* (formal plural) share the same verb forms.

The various parts of the set of verb forms, or conjugation, are *predictable* at several levels.

(i) Regular verbs

Regular verbs are those for which you can predict any form of any tense from the spelling of the infinitive (plus, of course, a knowledge of the rules!). Infinitives in Spanish end in **-ar, -er,** or **-ir** [4a], corresponding to the three main families of regular verbs, each with its own sets of forms and rules. Verbs for which some forms cannot be predicted in this way are *irregular*. Some of the most common Spanish verbs are irregular.

(ii) Imports

Verbs brought into Spanish from other languages and newly coined verbs tend to be regular **-ar** type of verbs.

dopar	dope, drug
esnifar	sniff (cocaine)
filmar	film

(iii)   Irregular verbs

Some irregular verbs have the same irregularities, so if you know one you can predict the forms of any of the others of that group. The so-called stem-changing verbs in Spanish fall into this category (**pensar, volver, pedir,** etc.).

There are also the following groups:

• those verbs that have a **-g-** in the first person singular form of the present indicative tense, and therefore throughout the present subjunctive (e.g., **pongo**);
• verbs with **-zc-** in the same place (e.g., **conozco**), and therefore throughout the present subjunctive;
• verbs with the irregular **pretérito grave** [10b(ix)].

(iv)   Compound verbs

With very few exceptions, compound verbs [10c] conjugate like their parent or base verb. Thus, for example, **contener, detener, mantener, obtener, retener, sostener** all behave as their parent verb **tener**.

10b   Major Groups of Verbs: How Are They Conjugated?

(i)   Conjugations

There are three *conjugations* or groups of verbs in Spanish, which take a set of endings according to their infinitives [4a]. The infinitives end in **-ar, -er,** or **-ir;** and the regular or predictable members of each family [10a] behave in the same way, having the same sets of verb endings and methods of forming each tense. In fact, a look at the verb tables [The Complete System of Tenses in Spanish (Section B)] will show that throughout the whole range of tenses, the endings for **-er** and **-ir** verbs are identical except for the following three endings, which differ only in the vowel contained in the ending:

-er verbs (e.g., **comer**)
present indicative: **comemos, coméis**
familiar plural imperative: **comed**

-ir verbs (e.g., **vivir**)
present indicative: **vivimos, vivís**
familiar plural imperative: **vivid**

For the other tenses and persons, they have identical endings.

(ii) *Spelling-change verbs*

These are verbs whose spelling has to be adjusted to maintain the correct consonant sound with some endings. Therefore this applies only to the written language, and it affects the last consonant(s) of the stem. The changes fall into the following main categories:

-ar verbs: The following changes are necessary before **-e-** throughout the present subjunctive tense, and in the first person singular form of the preterite tense.
* Stem ends in **-c-** → **-qu-**.
sacar (take out): **saque, saques,** etc.; **saqué**
* Stem ends in **-z-** → **-c-**.
empezar (begin): **empiece, empieces,** etc.; **empecé**
* Stem ends in **-g-** → **-gu-**.
pagar (pay): **pague, pagues,** etc.; **pagué**
* Stem ends in **-gu-** → **-gü-**.
averiguar (verify): **averigüe, averigües,** etc.; **averigüé**

-er and **-ir** verbs: The following changes are necessary before **-o** in the first person singular form of the present indicative tense and before **-a-** throughout the present subjunctive tense.
* Stem ends in **-gu-** → **-g-**.
seguir (follow): **sigo; siga, sigas,** etc.
* Stem ends in **-g-** → **-j-**.
escoger (choose): **escojo; escoja, escojas,** etc.
* Stem ends in **-c-** → **-z-**.
torcer (twist): **tuerzo; tuerza, tuerzas,** etc.

(iii) *-uir verbs*

Verbs ending in **-uir** have a **-y-** in the singular and third person plural forms of the present indicative tense, throughout the present and imperfect subjunctive tenses, in the third person form of the preterite tense (singular and plural), and in the gerund.

concluir (conclude)

present indicative:	**concluyo, concluyes, concluye, concluimos, concluís, concluyen**
present subjunctive:	**concluya, concluyas, concluya, concluyamos, concluyáis, concluyan**
preterite:	**concluí, concluiste, concluyó, concluimos, concluisteis, concluyeron**
imperfect subjunctive:	**concluyera / concluyese**
gerund:	**concluyendo**

(iv)   Accents

A small number of verbs with their stems ending in **-i-** or **-u-** need an accent to stress this vowel in the singular and third person plural forms of the present tense.

enviar (send)
present indicative: **envío, envías, envía, enviamos, enviáis, envían**
present subjunctive: **envíe, envíes, envíe, enviemos, enviéis, envíen**

actuar (act)
present indicative: **actúo, actúas, actúa, actuamos, actuáis, actúan**
present subjunctive: **actúe, actúes, actúe, actuemos, actuéis, actúen**

Note: **Desviar** (divert), **situar** (situate), **graduar** (grade), and **continuar** (continue) follow the same rules.

(v)   Stem-changing verbs

The biggest group of not quite regular, but predictably irregular verbs in Spanish are those that are variously known as radical-changing, root-changing, or stem-changing. In this book we refer to the part of the verb to which endings are added as the stem, so we shall use the term *stem-changing*.

You probably have noticed that many words in Spanish contain the diphthong **-ue-** or **-ie-,** where related words in English simply have **-o-** or **-e-**.

Spanish	*English*
puerto	port
muerto	mortuary
siete	septet
viento	ventilation

This stem change often happens in Spanish when in a conjugation, the syllable of the stem containing the original **-e-, -o-,** or **-u-** is stressed. When a verb is conjugated, the stress varies from stem to ending according to the person and tense, and in some verbs the stem changes when stressed.

There are three main types of stem-changing verbs:

Type 1: **-ar** and **-er** verbs
Stem change: **e** to **ie, o** to **ue,** and **u** to **ue** (**jugar** only).
The changes occur only in the present indicative and subjunctive tenses, where the stem is stressed, i.e., in all three singular forms and the third person plural form.

pensar (think)
present indicative: **pienso, piensas, piensa, piensan**
present subjunctive: **piense, pienses, piense, piensen**

volver (turn, return)
present indicative: **vuelvo, vuelves, vuelve, vuelven**
present subjunctive: **vuelva, vuelvas, vuelva, vuelvan**

jugar (play)
present indicative: **juego, juegas, juega, juegan**
present subjunctive: **juegue, juegues, juegue, jueguen**

> Type 2: **-ir** verbs
> Verbs of this type, like **mentir** (lie) or **dormir** (sleep), have the
> *same changes* in the *same places* as those of type 1. In addi-
> tion, the stem vowel changes from **e** to **i** and **o** to **u** in the fol-
> lowing tenses:

gerund: **mintiendo, durmiendo** [4b(i)]
present subjunctive: the first and second person plural forms [8a]
        mintamos, mintáis; durmamos, durmáis
preterite: the third person singular and plural forms [6b(iii)]
        mintió, mintieron; durmió, durmieron
imperfect subjunctive: throughout both forms of this tense [8b]
        mintiera/mintiese; durmiera/durmiese

> Type 3: **-ir** verbs
>
> Verbs of this type have the stem change in all the same places
> as type 2, but the change is *always* **e** to **i**.

pedir (request, ask for)
present indicative: **pido, pides, pide, piden**
present subjunctive: **pida, pidas, pida, pidamos, pidáis, pidan**
gerund: **pidiendo**
preterite: **pidió, pidieron**
imperfect subjunctive: **pidiera/pidiese**

(vi)   *-g- verbs*

> There is a group of verbs in which the stem of the present
> indicative contains **-g-** in the first person singular form only,
> and therefore throughout the present subjunctive tense. Some
> have a perfectly regular present indicative tense except for the
> first person form; others have stem changes [10b(v)].

hacer (do, make)
present indicative: **hago, haces, hace, hacemos, hacéis, hacen**
present subjunctive: **haga, hagas, haga, hagamos, hagáis, hagan**

tener (have)
present indicative: **tengo, tienes, tiene, tenemos, tenéis, tienen**
present subjunctive: **tenga, tengas, tenga, tengamos, tengáis, tengan**

The following verbs follow the same pattern:

caer (fall):   **caigo, caes**, etc.
poner (put):   **pongo, pones**, etc.
salir (go out):   **salgo, sales**, etc.
valer (be worth):   **valgo, vales**, etc.
decir (say):   **digo, dices, dice, decimos, decís, dicen**
oír (hear):   **oigo, oyes, oye, oímos, oís, oyen**

Note: Both the otherwise regular verbs and the stem-changing verbs keep
the **-g-** stem unchanged throughout the present subjunctive.

(vii)   *-zc- verbs*

Another sizable group with an irregular first person singular
form in the present indicative tense consists of verbs whose
infinitives end in **-ecer, -ocer,** and **-ucir**. The stem of the first
person form of the present indicative tense — and therefore all
of the present subjunctive tense — ends in **-zc-**.

parecer (seem)
present indicative: **parezco, pareces, parece, parecemos,
                           parecéis, parecen**
present subjunctive: **parezca, parezcas, parezca, parezcamos,
                           parezcáis, parezcan**

The following verbs follow the same pattern, just as many other verbs
ending in **-ecer** and all other verbs ending in **-ducir** do:

conocer	know, get to know	**lucir**	shine
reconocer	recognize	**conducir**	drive, conduct, lead
aparecer	appear	**producir**	produce
desaparecer	disappear	**reproducir**	reproduce
ofrecer	offer	**traducir**	translate
merecer	deserve		

(viii)   *-oy verbs*

In the following verbs, the first person singular form of the present indicative tense ends in **-oy**. The present subjunctive
tense is not affected by this.

dar (give):   **doy, das, da, damos, dais, dan**
estar (be):   **estoy, estás, está, estamos, estáis, están**

Note: Ir (go) is irregular, but the present tense is quite predictable once established:

voy, vas, va, vamos, vais, van

(ix)   *Pretérito grave*

A significant group of verbs have what is known as a **pretérito grave**. This refers to the fact that the first and third person singular preterite endings are not stressed and bear no accent. In addition, their set of preterite endings is a combination of the normal ones for **-ar** verbs (first and third person singular forms, but without accents) and **-er/-ir** verbs (all the rest).

tener (have):   **tuve, tuviste, tuvo, tuvimos, tuvisteis, tuvieron**

The following verbs also have a **pretérito grave**:

andar	→	**anduve**	**poner**	→	**puse**
caber	→	**cupe**	**querer**	→	**quise**
estar	→	**estuve**	**saber**	→	**supe**
haber	→	**hube**	**tener**	→	**tuve**
hacer	→	**hice**	**venir**	→	**vine**
poder	→	**pude**			

Note: Watch out for the following:

• The third person singular form of **hacer** is **hizo** in the preterite tense.
• When the stem of a **pretérito grave** ends in **-j-,** the third person plural ending is **-eron**.

decir	**dije**	**dijeron**
traer	**traje**	**trajeron**
conducir	**conduje**	**condujeron**

Compounds of the above verbs follow the same pattern [10c]. Therefore, **componer** follows **poner, mantener** follows **tener**. Also, all verbs ending in **-ducir** follow the same pattern as **conducir**.

10c   *Compound Verbs*

A compound verb is a verb with a prefix attached to it. It is conjugated in the same way as the original verb ('base verb'), but the meaning is usually different, according to the prefix. Some base verbs can take many more prefixes than others can and thus give rise to a whole list of verbs with different meanings. Some common prefixes are **con-, contra-, des-, dis-, inter-, mal-, pre-, pro-, re-,** and so forth.

(i)   Compound verb formation with some of these prefixes follows.

• Prefix **contra-** (against) + base verb

hacer (do, make)   →   **contrahacer** (counterfeit, copy)

• Prefix **des-** (often corresponding to English 'un-' or 'de') + base verb

atar (tie)	→	**desatar** (untie)
congelar (freeze)	→	**descongelar** (unfreeze, de-ice)
cubrir (cover)	→	**descubrir** (discover, uncover)
hacer (do)	→	**deshacer** (undo)

• Prefix **mal-** (meaning 'bad,' 'badly,' or 'evil') + base verb

gastar (spend)	→	**malgastar** (squander, waste)
decir (say)	→	**maldecir** (curse)

Note: The past participle of **maldecir** is **maldito.**

• Prefix **re-** (like English 're-,' but not used to the same extent to indicate repetition; often used to intensify) + base verb

hacer (do, make)	→	**rehacer** (remake)
vender (sell)	→	**revender** (resell)
llenar (fill)	→	**rellenar** (fill up, fill out)
mojar (wet)	→	**remojar** (soak, drench)
quemar (burn)	→	**requemar** (scorch, parch)

• Prefix **sobre-** (on, over) + base verb

venir (come)   →   **sobrevenir** (happen unexpectedly)

(ii)   **Poner** (put), **tener** (have), and **venir** (come) are among the verbs that can take many different prefixes.

• **Poner** has compounds that often correspond to English verbs ending in '-pose.'

componer	compose, mend
descomponerse	decompose, rot; break down (machine)
deponer	depose, lay down (arms, etc.)
imponer	impose
interponer	interpose
posponer	put behind, postpone

proponer	propose, suggest
reponer	replace, put back; reply
suponer	suppose
presuponer	presuppose

• **Tener** has compounds that correspond to English verbs ending in 'tain.'

contener	contain
detener	detain, stop
entretener	entertain, hold up, detain
mantener	maintain
retener	retain
sostener	sustain

• **Venir** has a number of compounds.

convenir	agree, suit
intervenir	intervene
provenir	come forth
sobrevenir	happen, occur (unexpectedly)

(iii) Finally, you can detect the many different prefixes in words that passed into Spanish as compound words directly from Latin. In the words that follow, Latin **ducĕre** (lead) combined with the different Latin prefixes to give us:

conducir	conduct, lead, drive
deducir	deduce
inducir	induce, induct
introducir	introduce, insert
producir	produce
reducir	reduce
reproducir	reproduce
seducir	seduce
traducir	translate

Similarly, you can see how Spanish **satisfacer** (satisfy) is a direct descendant of Latin **satisfacer,** a word made up of **satis** (enough) + **facĕre** (do, make). **Satisfacer** is conjugated like **hacer.**

11 Reflexive Verbs

11a   Reflexive Verbs in General

See section 2f for a general explanation of reflexive verbs. In addition to the verbs that are reflexive in English, Spanish treats many other verbs as reflexive. Many verbs can be used both as reflexive and as ordinary transitive verbs.

11b   Reflexive Pronouns

The full set of reflexive pronouns accompanying these verbs can be seen in this example of the present indicative tense of the reflexive verb **lavarse** (wash oneself):

me lavo	I wash myself
te lavas	you wash yourself (informal)
se lava	he/she washes him-/herself,
	you wash yourself (formal)
nos lavamos	we wash ourselves
os laváis	you wash yourselves (informal)
se lavan	they wash themselves,
	you wash yourselves (formal)

11c   Position of Reflexive Pronouns

Reflexive pronouns follow the same rules as other pronouns.

(A) They precede the verb:
• in all tenses of the indicative and the subjunctive;
• in all negative imperatives.

(B) They are joined to the end of the verb:
• in the gerund (optional);
• in all positive imperatives.

(C) With the infinitive, they can either precede the verb or be joined to the end of it.

Note: The stress pattern may require the use of a written accent to show that the stress stays the same.

¿*Te lavas* tú mismo, Paquito?	*Do you wash* all by *yourself*, Paquito?
No *te peines* así.	Don't *comb* your hair like that.
Estoy lavándome ahora mismo.	I'm *washing* right now.
¡*Levántense* inmediatamente!	Get up immediately!
Acuéstate a las diez.	Go to bed at ten.
Vamos a *bañarnos* en seguida. *Nos* vamos a *bañar* en seguida.	We are going *to take a bath* right now.

11d   Use of the Reflexive

Note that the reflexive form is often used in Spanish where one would use a possessive adjective in English.

Se lavaron las manos.	They washed *their* hands.
Mi novia *se pondrá el* vestido azul.	My girlfriend *will put on her* blue dress.

Note also the colloquial use of a reflexive form where normally the transitive form would be used, in order to intensify a statement or request.

Me comí todas las manzanas.	*I ate up* all the apples.

Note: The reflexive is often used to avoid a true passive [9b].

B
MODEL VERBS

41

Index of Model Verbs

Irregular verbs: *Number*

1 amar   love

Regular **-ar** verb

GERUND	PAST PARTICIPLE
amando	amado

ACTIVE VOICE

PRESENT INDICATIVE
amo
amas
ama
amamos
amáis
aman

PRESENT PERFECT
he amado
has amado
ha amado
hemos amado
habéis amado
han amado

PRESENT PROGRESSIVE
estoy amando
estás amando
está amando
estamos amando
estáis amando
están amando

IMPERFECT PROGRESSIVE
estaba amando
estabas amando
estaba amando
estábamos amando
estabais amando
estaban amando

IMPERFECT INDICATIVE
amaba
amabas
amaba
amábamos
amabais
amaban

PRETERITE
amé
amaste
amó
amamos
amasteis
amaron

PLUPERFECT
había amado
habías amado
había amado
habíamos amado
habíais amado
habían amado

PAST ANTERIOR
hube amado
hubiste amado
hubo amado
hubimos amado
hubisteis amado
hubieron amado

Note: See The Verb System in Spanish for explanations of the tenses. The important thing to note here is that all forms have the basic part, or stem, **am-**, which contains the meaning of the verb. Many tenses are simple tenses, in which endings are added to this stem to form just one word; other tenses are compound tenses, in which an auxiliary verb (helping verb) is used, in the appropriate tense and form, in

IMPERATIVE

(tú) ama	(vosotros) amad
(usted) ame	(ustedes) amen

FUTURE	FUTURE PERFECT
amaré	habré amado
amarás	habrás amado
amará	habrá amado
amaremos	habremos amado
amaréis	habréis amado
amarán	habrán amado

CONDITIONAL	CONDITIONAL PERFECT
amaría	habría/hubiera amado
amarías	habrías/hubieras amado
amaría	habría/hubiera amado
amaríamos	habríamos/hubiéramos amado
amaríais	habríais/hubierais amado
amarían	habrían/hubieran amado

PRESENT SUBJUNCTIVE	PERFECT SUBJUNCTIVE
ame	haya amado
ames	hayas amado
ame	haya amado
amemos	hayamos amado
améis	hayáis amado
amen	hayan amado

IMPERFECT SUBJUNCTIVE	PLUPERFECT SUBJUNCTIVE
amara/amase	hubiera/hubiese amado
amaras/amases	hubieras/hubieses amado
amara/amase	hubiera/hubiese amado
amáramos/amásemos	hubiéramos/hubiésemos amado
amarais/amaseis	hubierais/hubieseis amado
amaran/amasen	hubieran/hubiesen amado

front of the appropriate gerund or participle of the verb that contains the meaning. Remember that, in Spanish, the subject pronoun (**yo** = I, **tú** = you, etc.) is not normally needed because the verb endings are clear and distinct enough in both spoken and written forms; they are only needed for emphasis, contrast, or to avoid ambiguity.

1 amar love

For notes on other ways of expressing the passive, see The Verb System in Spanish.

PRESENT INDICATIVE
soy amado/a
eres amado/a
es amado/a
somos amados/as
sois amados/as
son amados/as

PRESENT PERFECT
he sido amado/a
has sido amado/a
ha sido amado/a
hemos sido amados/as
habéis sido amados/as
han sido amados/as

PRESENT PROGRESSIVE
estoy siendo amado/a
estás siendo amado/a
está siendo amado/a
estamos siendo amados/as
estáis siendo amados/as
están siendo amados/as

IMPERFECT PROGRESSIVE
estaba siendo amado/a
estabas siendo amado/a
estaba siendo amado/a
estábamos siendo amados/as
estabais siendo amados/as
estaban siendo amados/as

IMPERFECT INDICATIVE
era amado/a
eras amado/a
era amado/a
éramos amados/as
erais amados/as
eran amados/as

PRETERITE
fui amado/a
fuiste amado/a
fue amado/a
fuimos amados/as
fuisteis amados/as
fueron amados/as

PLUPERFECT
había sido amado/a
habías sido amado/a
había sido amado/a
habíamos sido amados/as
habíais sido amados/as
habían sido amados/as

PAST ANTERIOR
hube sido amado/a
hubiste sido amado/a
hubo sido amado/a
hubimos sido amados/as
hubisteis sido amados/as
hubieron sido amados/as

Jorge y Pedro *aman* a María, pero *ella* no *ama* a ninguno de los dos.

George and Peter *love* Mary, but she doesn't *love* either of them.

Si tus hermanos no te *amasen*, serías muy infeliz.

If your brothers and sisters *did*n't *love* you, you would be very unhappy.

FUTURE

seré amado/a
serás amado/a
será amado/a
seremos amados/as
seréis amados/as
serán amados/as

FUTURE PERFECT

habré sido amado/a
habrás sido amado/a
habrá sido amado/a
habremos sido amados/as
habréis sido amados/as
habrán sido amados/as

CONDITIONAL

sería amado/a
serías amado/a
sería amado/a
seríamos amados/as
seríais amados/as
serían amados/as

CONDITIONAL PERFECT

habría/hubiera sido amado/a
habrías/hubieras sido amado/a
habría/hubiera sido amado/a
habríamos/hubiéramos sido amados/as
habríais/hubierais sido amados/as
habrían/hubieran sido amados/as

PRESENT SUBJUNCTIVE

sea amado/a
seas amado/a
sea amado/a
seamos amados/as
seáis amados/as
sean amados/as

PERFECT SUBJUNCTIVE

haya amado/a
hayas amado/a
haya amado/a
hayamos amados/as
hayáis amados/as
hayan amados/as

IMPERFECT SUBJUNCTIVE

fuera/fuese amado/a
fueras/fueses amado/a
fuera/fuese amado/a
fuéramos/fuésemos amados/as

fuerais/fueseis amados/as
fueran/fuesen amados/as

PLUPERFECT SUBJUNCTIVE

hubiera/hubiese sido amado/a
hubieras/hubieses sido amado/a
hubiera/hubiese sido amado/a
hubiéramos/hubiésemos sido
amados/as
hubierais/hubieseis sido amados/as
hubieran/hubiesen sido amados/as

Mi maestra *amaba* los animales.   My teacher *loved* animals.

Ayer la *amabas;* aunque   Yesterday *you loved* her; even
hoy ya no la *amas*, tal vez   though today *you* do*n't love* her
mañana la *amarás* otra vez.   anymore, perhaps tomorrow *you*
   will love her again.

***Ellos se amaron* demasiado.**   *They loved each other* too much.

Regular **-ar** verb

GERUND	*PAST PARTICIPLE*
comprando	comprado

PRESENT INDICATIVE	*PRESENT PERFECT*
compro	he comprado
compras	has comprado
compra	ha comprado
compramos	hemos comprado
compráis	habéis comprado
compran	han comprado

PRESENT PROGRESSIVE	*IMPERFECT PROGRESSIVE*
estoy comprando	estaba comprando

IMPERFECT INDICATIVE	*PRETERITE*
compraba	compré
comprabas	compraste
compraba	compró
comprábamos	compramos
comprabais	comprasteis
compraban	compraron

Note: The number of verbs that follow the regular **-ar** verb conjugation is very large, so the verbs given below are only a small selection of the most useful verbs of this group. In the Verb Index you can find the main meanings of each verb, and one or two can also be found in the reflexive form, sometimes with different meanings, e.g., **llamarse** 'to be called.' Other verbs apparently in this group may actually be major irregular verbs, have minor spelling irregularities, or be stem-changing verbs. For these verbs you should consult the relevant section of this book. Note that some of the forms of the **-ar** conjugation are quite similar to those of the **-er** and **-ir** verbs, and that the following are the same:

- the first person singular (**yo**) ending in the present indicative tense;
- the auxiliary verbs for the compound tenses; and
- the formation and endings of the future tense.

Similar verbs

Only very few of the most commonly used **–ar** verbs are listed here.

ayudar	help	**dejar**	leave, let
bajar	go down	**entrar**	enter

IMPERATIVE
(tú) compra
(usted) compre

(vosotros) comprad
(ustedes) compren

PLUPERFECT
había comprado

PAST ANTERIOR
hube comprado

FUTURE
compraré

FUTURE PERFECT
habré comprado

CONDITIONAL
compraría

CONDITIONAL PERFECT
habría/hubiera comprado

PRESENT SUBJUNCTIVE
compre

PERFECT SUBJUNCTIVE
haya comprado

IMPERFECT SUBJUNCTIVE
comprara/comprase

PLUPERFECT SUBJUNCTIVE
hubiera/hubiese comprado

ganar	earn	**mirar**	look, see, watch
hablar	talk, speak	**pasar**	pass, spend
lavar	wash	**quedarse**	stay
levantarse	get up	**tomar**	take
llamar	call	**trabajar**	work
llevar	carry, wear		

¡Qué ambicioso!

What an ambitious guy!

—¿A qué hora *te levantas?*
"At what time *do you get up*?"
—A las siete.
"At seven."
—¿Por qué tan temprano?
"Why so early?"
—Quiero *trabajar* mucho.
"I want to *work* a lot."
—¿Por qué?
"Why?"
—Para *ganar* mucho dinero. Un día voy a *comprarme* una casa muy grande, *pasaré* mis vacaciones en Europa, y...
"To *earn* lots of money. One day I am going to *buy* a very big house, *I* will *spend* my vacations in Europe, and ...
¡entonces me voy a *quedar* en la cama hasta mediodía! ¡Es por eso que ahora *trabajo* tanto!
then *I* will *stay* in bed until noon! That's why *I'm working* so hard now!"

49

3 comer   eat

Regular **-er** verb

GERUND	*PAST PARTICIPLE*
comiendo	comido

PRESENT INDICATIVE	*PRESENT PERFECT*
como	he comido
comes	has comido
come	ha comido
comemos	hemos comido
coméis	habéis comido
comen	han comido

PRESENT PROGRESSIVE	*IMPERFECT PROGRESSIVE*
estoy comiendo	estaba comiendo

IMPERFECT INDICATIVE	*PRETERITE*
comía	comí
comías	comiste
comía	comió
comíamos	comimos
comíais	comisteis
comían	comieron

Similar verbs

Only some of the most commonly used **-er** verbs are listed here.

aprender	learn	**sorprender**	surprise; catch out
beber	drink	**suceder**	succeed, happen
correr	run	**suspender**	give a failing grade
coser	sew	**temer**	fear
deber	owe, must	**toser**	cough
prometer	promise	**vender**	sell

Note: Although the **-er** group of verbs is a large one, many are irregular or are subject to spelling changes. These verbs appear in the appropriate sections of this book; those appearing above are entirely regular. Many of these verbs can be used in both reflexive and non-relexive form; the list gives the most commonly used form. Note that some of the forms of the **-er** conjugation are very similar to those of the **-ar** verbs, and that the following are the same as for both **-ar** and **-ir** verbs:
   • the first person singular (**yo**) ending in the present indicative tense;
   • the auxiliary verbs for the compound tenses; and
   • the formation and endings of the future tense.

IMPERATIVE

(tú) come (vosotros) comed
(usted) coma (ustedes) coman

PLUPERFECT	**PAST ANTERIOR**
había comido	hube comido

FUTURE	**FUTURE PERFECT**
comeré	habré comido

CONDITIONAL	**CONDITIONAL PERFECT**
comería	habría/hubiera comido

PRESENT SUBJUNCTIVE	**PERFECT SUBJUNCTIVE**
coma	haya comido

IMPERFECT SUBJUNCTIVE	**PLUPERFECT SUBJUNCTIVE**
comprara/comprase	hubiera/hubiese comido

The following forms are the same as for **-ir** verbs:
- four out of six of the present indicative forms;
- the gerund (or present participle) and the past participle;
- the preterite and the imperfect indicative tenses

¡Qué alumno más malo!	What an awful pupil!
—¿Qué le *sucede* a Sánchez? ¡No *aprende* nada!	"What's *happening* to Sánchez? *He learns* nothing!"
—Es que pasa todo su tiempo libre *vendiendo* periódicos en la calle. Quiere comprar un automóvil, por eso *debe* ganar dinero....	"He's spending all his free time *selling* newspapers on the street. He wants to buy a car, so *he has to* earn money...."
—Ayer, Sánchez *prometió* que, de aquí en adelante, *aprenderá* todo muy bien.	"Yesterday, Sánchez *promised* that, from now on, *he will learn* everything well."
—Espero que sí. Si no, *temo* que el profesor lo va a *suspender*.	"I hope so. If not, *I fear* the teacher is going to *give him a failing grade*."

4 vivir   live

Regular **-ir** verb

GERUND	**PAST PARTICIPLE**
viviendo	vivido

PRESENT INDICATIVE	**PRESENT PERFECT**
vivo	he vivido
vives	has vivido
vive	ha vivido
vivimos	hemos vivido
vivís	habéis vivido
viven	han vivido

PRESENT PROGRESSIVE	**IMPERFECT PROGRESSIVE**
estoy viviendo	estaba viviendo

IMPERFECT INDICATIVE	**PRETERITE**
vivía	viví
vivías	viviste
vivía	vivió
vivíamos	vivimos
vivíais	vivisteis
vivían	vivieron

Similar verbs

Only some of the most commonly used **-ir** verbs are listed here.

aburrir	bore	**dividir**	divide
admitir	accept	**partir**	depart, split
asistir	attend, assist	**persuadir**	persuade
consistir	consist	**sobrevivir**	survive
convivir	live together, coexist	**subir**	go up, raise
decidir	decide	**sufrir**	suffer
discutir	discuss	**unir**	unite

Note: The **-ir** group of verbs is very large, but many are irregular or are subject to spelling changes. These verbs appear in the appropriate sections of this book; those listed above are entirely regular. Many of the listed verbs can be used in both reflexive and nonreflexive forms; the most commonly used forms are given in the above list. Note that some of the forms of the **-ir** conjugation are similar to or the same as those of the **-ar** and **-er** verbs. The following are the same as for both **-ar** and **-er** verbs:
  • the first person singular (**yo**) ending in the present indicative tense;
  • the auxiliary verbs for the compound tenses; and
  • the formation and endings of the future tense.

IMPERATIVE
(tú) vive
(usted) viva

(vosotros) vivid
(ustedes) vivan

PLUPERFECT
había vivido

PAST ANTERIOR
hube vivido

FUTURE
viviré

FUTURE PERFECT
habré vivido

CONDITIONAL
viviría

CONDITIONAL PERFECT
habría/hubiera vivido

PRESENT SUBJUNCTIVE
viva

PERFECT SUBJUNCTIVE
haya vivido

IMPERFECT SUBJUNCTIVE
viviera/viviese

PLUPERFECT SUBJUNCTIVE
hubiera/hubiese vivido

The following forms are the same as for **-er** verbs:
• four out of six of the present indicative forms;
• the gerund (or present participle) and the past participle;
• the preterite and the imperfect indicative tenses.

¡Qué muchacho más difícil!

What a difficult guy!

Tomás es un joven que *se aburre* muy fácilmente. Su único interés real *consiste* en leer y escribir, y en hablar sobre lo que lee y escribe. Sus amigos *sufren* mucho por esto, porque nunca pueden *persuadirlo* para que salga con ellos. Además, él siempre quiere que la casa esté tranquila. Es muy difícil *vivir* con un muchacho como Tomás, pero sus amigos lo quieren. Por eso *han decidido* que permanecerán juntos y no se separarán.

Thomas is a young man who *gets bored* very easily. His only real interest *consists* of reading and writing and of talking about what he reads and writes. His friends *suffer* a lot out of this, because they can never *persuade him* to go out with them. Besides, he always wants the house to be quiet. It's hard *to live* with a guy like Thomas, but his friends love him. Therefore *they have decided* that they will stay together and will not separate.

5 sacar   take out

-ar verbs: c → qu

GERUND	PAST PARTICIPLE
sacando	sacado

PRESENT INDICATIVE	PRESENT PERFECT
saco	he sacado

PRESENT PROGRESSIVE	IMPERFECT PROGRESSIVE
estoy sacando	estaba sacando

IMPERFECT INDICATIVE	PRETERITE
sacaba	saqué
	sacaste
	sacó
	sacamos
	sacasteis
	sacaron

PLUPERFECT	PAST ANTERIOR
había sacado	hube sacado

Similar verbs

aparcar	park	**buscar**	look for, search
aparcar	park	**buscar**	look for, search
aplicar	apply	**confiscar**	confiscate
arrancar	start up	**criticar**	criticize
atacar	attack	**tocar**	touch, play *(instrument)*
atracar	assault, mug; moor, tie up		

Note: The **-c-** changes to **-qu-** before verb endings beginning with an **-e-**, in order to preserve the sound. In all other respects these verbs are regular. There are verbs other than the ones above that have the c → qu change, but they are not listed here because they are stem-changing verbs.

IMPERATIVE

(tú) saca	(vosotros) sacad
(usted) saque	(ustedes) saquen

FUTURE
sacaré

FUTURE PERFECT
habré sacado

CONDITIONAL
sacaría

CONDITIONAL PERFECT
habría/hubiera sacado

PRESENT SUBJUNCTIVE
saque
saques
saque
saquemos
saquéis
saquen

PERFECT SUBJUNCTIVE
haya sacado

IMPERFECT SUBJUNCTIVE
sacara/sacase

PLUPERFECT SUBJUNCTIVE
hubiera/hubiese sacado

El atraco

El sábado pasado, fui víctima de un atraco. Al llegar al centro ciudad, *busqué* un sitio para dejar el coche. Por fin *aparqué* en una calle oscura. Cuando bajé del coche, alguien me *tocó* en la espalda con una navaja. El ladrón me dijo: "*Saque* el monedero". En lugar del monedero, *saqué* mi alarma personal. Con el ruido, *el hombre que me atacó* se fue corriendo.

The mugging

Last Saturday I was the victim of a mugging. When I got downtown, *I looked for* a place to park the car. Finally, *I parked* on a dark street. As I got out of the car, someone *touched* me in the back with a knife. The mugger said, "*Take out* your wallet." Instead of the wallet, *I took out* my personal alarm. With the noise, *the attacker* ran off.

6 cazar

hunt, chase

-ar verbs: **z** → **c**

GERUND	PAST PARTICIPLE
cazando	cazado

PRESENT INDICATIVE	PRESENT PERFECT
cazo	he cazado

PRESENT PROGRESSIVE	IMPERFECT PROGRESSIVE
estoy cazando	estaba cazando

IMPERFECT INDICATIVE	PRETERITE
cazaba	cacé
	cazaste
	cazó
	cazamos
	cazasteis
	cazaron

PLUPERFECT	PAST ANTERIOR
había cazado	hube cazado

Similar verbs

abrazar	hug, embrace	**lanzar**	launch, throw
avergonzarse	be ashamed	**rezar**	pray

Note: The **-z-** changes to **-c-** before verb endings beginning with an **-e-**. In all other respects these verbs are regular. There are quite a few verbs other than the ones listed above that have the **z** → **c** change, but they are not listed here because they are stem-changing verbs.

IMPERATIVE

(tú) caza   (vosotros) cazad
(usted) cace   (ustedes) cacen

FUTURE	**FUTURE PERFECT**
cazaré	habré cazado

CONDITIONAL	**CONDITIONAL PERFECT**
cazaría	habría/hubiera cazado

PRESENT SUBJUNCTIVE   **PERFECT SUBJUNCTIVE**

cace   haya cazado
caces
cace
cacemos
cacéis
cacen

IMPERFECT SUBJUNCTIVE   **PLUPERFECT SUBJUNCTIVE**

cazara/cazase   hubiera/hubiese cazado

Me avergoncé de no pasar el examen.

I was ashamed of failing the exam.

Mi madre *estaba rezando* en la iglesia cuando *lanzaron* una bomba en un edificio cercano.

My mother *was praying* in church when *they threw* a bomb into a nearby building.

***Él* nos *abrazó* y partió.**

He embraced us and left.

No *te avergüences de* abrazar a alguien en público.

Don't be ashamed of hugging someone in public.

-ar verbs: **g** → **gu**

GERUND	*PAST PARTICIPLE*
pagando	pagado

PRESENT INDICATIVE	*PRESENT PERFECT*
pago	he pagado
PRESENT PROGRESSIVE	*IMPERFECT PROGRESSIVE*
estoy pagando	estaba pagando
IMPERFECT INDICATIVE	*PRETERITE*
pagaba	pagué
	pagaste
	pagó
	pagamos
	pagasteis
	pagaron
PLUPERFECT	*PAST ANTERIOR*
había pagado	hube pagado

Similar verbs

apagar	put out, switch off, turn off	**obligar**	oblige; force
llegar	arrive; reach		

Note: The **-g-** changes to **-gu-** before verb endings beginning with **-e-**, in order to preserve the sound. In all other respects these verbs are regular. There are quite a few verbs other than the ones listed above that have the **g** → **gu** change, but are not listed here because they are stem-changing verbs.

IMPERATIVE
(tú) paga
(usted) pague

(vosotros) pagad
(ustedes) paguen

FUTURE
pagaré

FUTURE PERFECT
habré pagado

CONDITIONAL
pagaría

CONDITIONAL PERFECT
habría/hubiera pagado

PRESENT SUBJUNCTIVE
pague
pagues
pague
paguemos
paguéis
paguen

PERFECT SUBJUNCTIVE
haya pagado

IMPERFECT SUBJUNCTIVE
pagara/pagase

PLUPERFECT SUBJUNCTIVE
hubiera/hubiese pagado

Espero que me *pagues* pronto.

I hope *you will pay* me soon.

***Paguen* la cuenta, señores; no me *obliguen* a llamar a la policía.**

Pay the bill, gentlemen; *do* not *force* me to call the police.

Si los bomberos *hubieran llegado* a tiempo, *habrían apagado* el incendio.

If the firemen *had arrived* on time, *they would have put out* the fire.

-ar verbs: **gu** → **gü**

GERUND	*PAST PARTICIPLE*
averiguando	averiguado

PRESENT INDICATIVE	*PRESENT PERFECT*
averiguo	he averiguado

PRESENT PROGRESSIVE	*IMPERFECT PROGRESSIVE*
estoy averiguando	estaba averiguando

IMPERFECT INDICATIVE	*PRETERITE*
averiguaba	averigüé
	averiguaste
	averiguó
	averiguamos
	averiguasteis
	averiguaron

PLUPERFECT	*PAST ANTERIOR*
había averiguado	hube averiguado

Similar verbs

amortiguar   deaden, muffle   **apaciguar**   pacify, appease

Note: The **-gu-** changes to **-gü-** before verb endings beginning with an **-e-**, in order to preserve the sound. In all other respects these verbs are regular.

IMPERATIVE

(tú) averigua   (vosotros) averiguad
(usted) averigüe   (ustedes) averigüen

FUTURE   **FUTURE PERFECT**
averiguaré   habré averiguado

CONDITIONAL   **CONDITIONAL PERFECT**
averiguaría   habría/hubiera averiguado

PRESENT SUBJUNCTIVE   **PERFECT SUBJUNCTIVE**
averigüe   haya averiguado
averigües
averigüe
averigüemos
averigüéis
averigüen

IMPERFECT SUBJUNCTIVE   **PLUPERFECT SUBJUNCTIVE**
averiguara/averiguase   hubiera/hubiese averiguado

Ayer *averigüé* dónde se obtiene la licencia de conducir.

Yesterday *I found out* where you can get a driver's license.

Las paredes *amortiguaban* los ruidos.

The walls *muffled* the noises.

Apacigüe su sed con agua, no con vino.

Quench your thirst with water, not with wine.

9 vencer   win; defeat

-er and **-ir** verbs: **c → z**

GERUND	PAST PARTICIPLE
venciendo	vencido

PRESENT INDICATIVE	PRESENT PERFECT
venzo	he vencido
vences	
vence	
vencemos	
vencéis	
vencen	

PRESENT PROGRESSIVE	IMPERFECT PROGRESSIVE
estoy venciendo	estaba venciendo

IMPERFECT INDICATIVE	PRETERITE
vencía	vencí

PLUPERFECT	PAST ANTERIOR
había vencido	hube vencido

Similar verbs

convencer	convince	**esparcir**	scatter, spread
ejercer	exercise, exert	**mecer**	rock, swing

Note: The **-c-** changes to **-z-** before verb endings beginning with an **-a-** or an **-o-**, in order to preserve the sound. In all other respects these verbs are regular. There are verbs other than the ones listed above that have the **c → z** change, but they are not listed here because they are stem-changing verbs.

IMPERATIVE

(tú) vence	(vosotros) venced
(usted) venza	(ustedes) venzan

FUTURE
venceré

FUTURE PERFECT
habré vencido

CONDITIONAL
vencería

CONDITIONAL PERFECT
habría/hubiera vencido

PRESENT SUBJUNCTIVE
venza
venzas
venza
venzamos
venzáis
venzan

PERFECT SUBJUNCTIVE
haya vencido

IMPERFECT SUBJUNCTIVE
venciera/venciese

PLUPERFECT SUBJUNCTIVE
hubiera/hubiese vencido

Yo no *ejerzo* ninguna influencia sobre mi hermano.	*I exert* no influence on my brother.
Esparza las semillas sobre la tierra.	*Scatter* the seeds on the ground.
Finalmente la *convencí* para que se quedara en casa con su madre.	*I* finally *convinced* her to stay home with her mother.
No me *convences* ...	*You* don't *convince* me. . . .
Meza la cuna de su bebé con cuidado.	*Rock* your baby's cradle carefully.

10 distinguir distinguish; make out

-er and **-ir** verbs: **gu** → **g**

GERUND	PAST PARTICIPLE
distinguiendo	distinguido

PRESENT INDICATIVE	PRESENT PERFECT
distingo	he distinguido
distingues	
distingue	
distinguimos	
distinguís	
distinguen	

PRESENT PROGRESSIVE	IMPERFECT PROGRESSIVE
estoy distinguiendo	estaba distinguiendo

IMPERFECT INDICATIVE	PRETERITE
distinguía	distinguí

PLUPERFECT	PAST ANTERIOR
había distinguido	hube distinguido

Similar verb

extinguir   extinguish, put out

Note: The **-gu-** changes to **-g-** before verb endings beginning with an **-o-** or an **-a-**. In all other respects these verbs are regular. There are verbs other than **distinguir** and **extinguir** that have the **g** → **gu** change, but they are not listed here because they are stem-changing verbs.

IMPERATIVE

(tú) distingue   (vosotros) distinguid
(usted) distinga   (ustedes) distingan

FUTURE	**FUTURE PERFECT**
distinguiré	habré distinguido

CONDITIONAL	**CONDITIONAL PERFECT**
distinguiría	habría/hubiera distinguido

PRESENT SUBJUNCTIVE   **PERFECT SUBJUNCTIVE**

distinga   haya distinguido
distingas
distinga
distingamos
distingáis
distingan

IMPERFECT SUBJUNCTIVE   **PLUPERFECT SUBJUNCTIVE**

distinguiera/distinguiese   hubiera/hubiese distinguido

Hace falta que *distingas* entre los dos.

You need to *distinguish* between the two of them.

Los bomberos *extinguieron* el fuego.

The firefighters *extinguished* the fire.

Sin mis lentes, no *distingo* bien las cosas.

Without my glasses, I don't *make out* things well.

65

11 coger   take, catch

-er and **-ir** verbs: **g** → **j**

GERUND	PAST PARTICIPLE
cogiendo	cogido

PRESENT INDICATIVE	PRESENT PERFECT
cojo	he cogido
coges	
coge	
cogemos	
cogéis	
cogen	

PRESENT PROGRESSIVE	IMPERFECT PROGRESSIVE
estoy cogiendo	estaba cogiendo

IMPERFECT INDICATIVE	PRETERITE
cogía	cogí

PLUPERFECT	PAST ANTERIOR
había cogido	hube cogido

Similar verbs

acoger	welcome	**proteger**	protect
escoger	choose	**restringir**	restrict
fingir	feign, pretend		

Note: The **-g-** changes to **-j-** before verb endings beginning with an **-a-** or an **-o-** in order to preserve the sound. In all other respects these verbs are regular. There are verbs other than the ones listed above that have the **g** → **j** change, but they are not listed here because they are stem-changing verbs.

IMPERATIVE

(tú) coge	(vosotros) coged
(usted) coja	(ustedes) cojan

FUTURE
cogeré

FUTURE PERFECT
habré cogido

CONDITIONAL
cogería

CONDITIONAL PERFECT
habría/hubiera cogido

PRESENT SUBJUNCTIVE
coja
cojas
coja
cojamos
cojáis
cojan

PERFECT SUBJUNCTIVE
haya cogido

IMPERFECT SUBJUNCTIVE
cogiera/cogiese

PLUPERFECT SUBJUNCTIVE
hubiera/hubiese cogido

¡*Cojan* todo lo que puedan!

Take everything you can!

Cuando voy al cine, siempre *escojo* una película extranjera.

When I go to the movies, *I* always *choose* a foreign film.

Nos *acogieron* en su hogar como si fueramos parte de su familia.

They welcomed us in their home as if we were part of their family.

Restringe tus gastos, y *protegerás* tu futuro.

Restrict your expenses, and you *will protect* your future.

-uir verbs: **i → y**

GERUND	PAST PARTICIPLE
huyendo	huido

PRESENT INDICATIVE	PRESENT PERFECT
huyo	he huido
huyes	
huye	
huimos	
huís	
huyen	

PRESENT PROGRESSIVE	IMPERFECT PROGRESSIVE
estoy huyendo	estaba huyendo

IMPERFECT INDICATIVE	PRETERITE
huía	huí
	huiste
	huyó
	huimos
	huisteis
	huyeron

Similar verbs

concluir	conclude	**disminuir**	diminish, lessen
construir	build, construct	**excluir**	exclude
destruir	destroy	**incluir**	include
distribuir	distribute	**influir**	influence

Note: The **-i-** is replaced by **-y-** to avoid having three vowels together. In all other respects these verbs are regular.

IMPERATIVE
(tú) huye   (vosotros) huid
(usted) huya   (ustedes) huyan

PLUPERFECT   PAST ANTERIOR
había huido   hube huido

FUTURE   FUTURE PERFECT
huiré   habré huido

CONDITIONAL   CONDITIONAL PERFECT
huiría   habría/hubiera huido

PRESENT SUBJUNCTIVE   PERFECT SUBJUNCTIVE
huya   haya huido
huyas
huya
huyamos
huyáis
huyan

IMPERFECT SUBJUNCTIVE   PLUPERFECT SUBJUNCTIVE
huyera/huyese   hubiera/hubiese huido

¡*Huye*, que ya viene la policía!   *Run*, the police are coming!

Los moros *construyeron*   The Moors *built*
esta casa.   this house.

El juez *concluyó* que el reo   The judge *concluded* that the
era inocente.   prisoner was innocent.

Los impuestos *están incluidos*   The taxes *are included*
en el precio.   in the price.

13 leer   read

-eer verbs: take a **-y-** between vowels

GERUND	*PAST PARTICIPLE*
leyendo	leído

PRESENT INDICATIVE	*PRESENT PERFECT*
leo	he leído

PRESENT PROGRESSIVE	*IMPERFECT PROGRESSIVE*
estoy leyendo	estaba leyendo

IMPERFECT INDICATIVE	*PRETERITE*
leía	leí
	leíste
	leyó
	leímos
	leísteis
	leyeron

PLUPERFECT	*PAST ANTERIOR*
había leído	hube leído

Similar verbs

creer   believe   **poseer**   possess, own, have

Note: The **-i-** is replaced by **-y-** to avoid having three vowels together in
          certain forms (including the imperfect subjunctive); in others the
          -i- takes a written accent to keep the stress in the correct place. In all
          other respects these verbs are regular. Note that **caer** (fall) and **oír**
          (hear) have a similar spelling change, but are also irregular in other
          ways.

IMPERATIVE

(tú) lee	(vosotros) leed
(usted) lea	(ustedes) lean

FUTURE	**FUTURE PERFECT**
leeré	habré leído

CONDITIONAL	**CONDITIONAL PERFECT**
leería	habría/hubiera leído

PRESENT SUBJUNCTIVE   **PERFECT SUBJUNCTIVE**

lea   haya leído
leas
lea
leamos
leáis
lean

IMPERFECT SUBJUNCTIVE	**PLUPERFECT SUBJUNCTIVE**
leyera/leyese	hubiera/hubiese leído

¿*Leyeron* la noticias sobre la guerra?	*Did you read* the news about the war?
***Ellos* no *creían* lo que estaban *leyendo*.**	*They didn't believe what they were reading.*
Roberto *tenía* dos defectos: nunca *leía*, y no *creía* en nada.	Robert *had* two faults: *he* never *read*, and *he didn't believe* in anything.

14 enviar   send

verbs with stressed weak vowel: **i → í**

GERUND	PAST PARTICIPLE
enviando	enviado

PRESENT INDICATIVE	PRESENT PERFECT
envío	he enviado
envías	
envía	
enviamos	
enviáis	
envían	

PRESENT PROGRESSIVE	IMPERFECT PROGRESSIVE
estoy enviando	estaba enviando

IMPERFECT INDICATIVE	PRETERITE
enviaba	envié

PLUPERFECT	PAST ANTERIOR
había enviado	hube enviado

Similar verbs

confiar	confide, entrust	**fiarse**	trust
criar	rear, bring up, raise	**guiar**	guide
desafiar	challenge, defy	**liar**	bind, tie
desviar	divert, detour	**vaciar**	empty

Note: These **-iar** verbs require an accent on the **-i-** when it is stressed in a conjugation, as shown above. The endings are all regular. Note also that some verbs require an accent on the **-i-** of the stem when it is stressed **aislar** (isolate) and **prohibir** (prohibit).

IMPERATIVE

(tú) envía	(vosotros) enviad
(usted) envíe	(ustedes) envíen

FUTURE	**FUTURE PERFECT**
enviaré	habré enviado
PERFECT	**CONDITIONAL PERFECT**
enviaría	habría / hubiera enviado
PRESENT SUBJUNCTIVE	**PERFECT SUBJUNCTIVE**
envíe	haya enviado
envíes	
envíe	
enviemos	
enviéis	
envíen	
IMPERFECT SUBJUNCTIVE	**PLUPERFECT SUBJUNCTIVE**
enviara / enviase	hubiera / hubiese enviado

Pepe *criaba* ovejas en Alcalá.	Pepe *used to raise* sheep in Alcalá.
***Vacíen* sus bolsillos.**	*Empty* your pockets.
Mi amigo me *confió* un secreto.	My friend *told* me a secret.
Te *desafío* a una carrera.	*I challenge* you to a race.

verbs with stressed weak vowel: **u** → **ú**

GERUND	*PAST PARTICIPLE*
actuando	actuado

PRESENT INDICATIVE	*PRESENT PERFECT*
actúo	he actuado
actúas	
actúa	
actuamos	
actuáis	
actúan	

PRESENT PROGRESSIVE	*IMPERFECT PROGRESSIVE*
estoy actuando	estaba actuando

IMPERFECT INDICATIVE	*PRETERITE*
actuaba	actué

PLUPERFECT	*PAST ANTERIOR*
había actuado	hube actuado

Similar verbs

continuar	continue	**exceptuar**	except
devaluar	devalue	**insinuar**	insinuate, suggest
evaluar	evaluate	**perpetuar**	perpetuate

Note: The accent is needed on certain forms to keep the stress in the correct place. The endings are regular. The verb **reunir(se)** (join) needs an accent on the **-u-** when it is stressed.

IMPERATIVE

(tú) actúa   (vosotros) actuad
(usted) actúe   (ustedes) actúen

FUTURE	**FUTURE PERFECT**
actuaré	habré actuado

CONDITIONAL	**CONDITIONAL PERFECT**
actuaría	habría/hubiera actuado

PRESENT SUBJUNCTIVE	**PERFECT SUBJUNCTIVE**
actúe	haya actuado
actúes	
actúe	
actuemos	
actuéis	
actúen	

IMPERFECT SUBJUNCTIVE	**PLUPERFECT SUBJUNCTIVE**
actuara/actuase	hubiera/hubiese actuado

Pese a que se lo *insinúo* siempre, Ana *actúa* como si no entendiera.

Although *I* always *suggest* it to her, Anna *acts* as if she didn't understand.

Antes de que el gobierno *devalúe* la moneda, es necesario que los economistas *evalúen* los efectos.

Before the government *devalues* the currency, it is necessary that the economists *evaluate* the effects.

***Continúa* ensayando hasta que *actúes* bien.**

Continue rehearsing until you *act* well.

16 zambullir(se) dive, plunge (into water); dip

verbs whose stems end in **-ll-**

GERUND	PAST PARTICIPLE
zambullendo	zambullido

PRESENT INDICATIVE	PRESENT PERFECT
zambullo	he zambullido

PRESENT PROGRESSIVE	IMPERFECT PROGRESSIVE
estoy zambullendo	estaba zambullendo

IMPERFECT INDICATIVE	PRETERITE
zambullía	zambullí
	zambulliste
	zambulló
	zambullimos
	zambullisteis
	zambulleron

PLUPERFECT	PAST ANTERIOR
había zambullido	hube zambullido

Similar verbs

engullir   gobble, gulp   **escabullirse**   slip away

Note: Due to the **-ll-**, the **-i-** disappears in certain forms, as shown above, when followed by another — stressed — vowel.

IMPERATIVE

(tú) zambulle

(usted) zambulla

(vosotros) zambullid

(ustedes) zambullan

FUTURE

zambulliré

FUTURE PERFECT

habré zambullido

CONDITIONAL

zambulliría

CONDITIONAL PERFECT

habría / hubiera zambullido

PRESENT SUBJUNCTIVE

zambulla

PERFECT SUBJUNCTIVE

haya zambullido

IMPERFECT SUBJUNCTIVE

zambullera / zambullese

zambulleras / zambulleses

zambullera / zambullese

zambulléramos / zambullésemos

zambullerais / zambulleseis

zambulleran / zambullesen

PLUPERFECT SUBJUNCTIVE

hubiera / hubiese zambullido

El ladrón *se escabulló* con las joyas.

The thief *slipped away* with the jewels.

Están zambulléndose en la piscina.

They're diving into the swimming pool.

¡No *engullas* la comida!

Don't *gobble* the food!

17 gruñir   grunt

verbs whose stems end in **-ñ-**

GERUND	PAST PARTICIPLE
gruñendo	gruñido

PRESENT INDICATIVE	PRESENT PERFECT
gruño	he gruñido

PRESENT PROGRESSIVE	IMPERFECT PROGRESSIVE
estoy gruñendo	estaba gruñendo

IMPERFECT INDICATIVE	PRETERITE
gruñía	gruñí
	gruñiste
	gruñó
	gruñimos
	gruñisteis
	gruñeron

PLUPERFECT	PAST ANTERIOR
había gruñido	hube gruñido

Similar verbs

ceñir	gird, surround, skirt	tañer	play, pluck (*instrument*)
reñir	scold, quarrel	teñir	dye

Note: Due to the **-ñ-**, the **-i-** disappears in certain forms, as shown above, when followed by another — stressed — vowel.

IMPERATIVE
(tú) gruñe
(usted) gruña

(vosotros) gruñid
(ustedes) gruñan

FUTURE
gruñiré

FUTURE PERFECT
habré gruñido

CONDITIONAL
gruñiría

CONDITIONAL PERFECT
habría/hubiera gruñido

PRESENT SUBJUNCTIVE
gruña

PERFECT SUBJUNCTIVE
haya gruñido

IMPERFECT SUBJUNCTIVE
gruñera/gruñese
gruñeras/gruñeses
gruñera/gruñese
gruñéramos/gruñésemos
gruñerais/gruñeseis
gruñeran/gruñesen

PLUPERFECT SUBJUNCTIVE
hubiera/hubiese gruñido

La profesora *riñó* a las chicas.   The teacher *scolded* the girls.

Los músicos *tañeron* suavemente sus arpas.   The musicians *plucked* their harps softly.

Mi padre *gruñe* cada vez que se enoja.   My father *grunts* whenever he is upset.

18 asir(se)　　　seize; grasp; grab

forms with a **-g-**

GERUND	PAST PARTICIPLE
asiendo	asido

PRESENT INDICATIVE	PRESENT PERFECT
asgo	he asido
ases	
ase	
asimos	
asís	
asen	

PRESENT PROGRESSIVE	IMPERFECT PROGRESSIVE
estoy asiendo	estaba asiendo

IMPERFECT INDICATIVE	PRETERITE
asía	así

PLUPERFECT	PAST ANTERIOR
había asido	hube asido

Note:　In practice, the forms containing a **-g-** should not be used. To avoid them, use a different verb.

IMPERATIVE

(tú) ase

(usted) asga

(vosotros) asid

(ustedes) asgan

FUTURE	**FUTURE PERFECT**
asiré	habré asido
CONDITIONAL	**CONDITIONAL PERFECT**
asiría	habría/hubiera asido
PRESENT SUBJUNCTIVE	**PERFECT SUBJUNCTIVE**
asga	haya asido
asgas	
asga	
asgamos	
asgáis	
asgan	
IMPERFECT SUBJUNCTIVE	**PLUPERFECT SUBJUNCTIVE**
asiera/asiese	hubiera/hubiese asido

Me *así* a la barra para *evitar* caer.	*I grabbed* the bar to avoid falling.
¡*Ásete* a esa rama!	*Grasp* that branch!

19 pensar   think

type 1 stem-changing verb **e** → **ie**

GERUND	PAST PARTICIPLE
pensando	pensado

PRESENT INDICATIVE	PRESENT PERFECT
pienso	he pensado
piensas	
piensa	
pensamos	
pensáis	
piensan	

PRESENT PROGRESSIVE	IMPERFECT PROGRESSIVE
estoy pensando	estaba pensando

IMPERFECT INDICATIVE	PRETERITE
pensaba	pensé
	pensaste
	pensó
	pensamos
	pensasteis
	pensaron

Similar verbs

Only a very small selection of **e** → **ie** stem-changing verbs is listed here.

cerrar	close	**encender**	light, switch on
comenzar	commence, start	**entender**	understand
empezar	begin	**sentarse**	sit down

Note: These verbs are type 1 stem-changing verbs. They are irregular only in the present indicative and present subjunctive tenses, and thus also in the imperative forms except for the **vosotros** form (**pensad**). What happens is that the **-e-** in the stem changes to **-ie-** in those forms in which the stress falls on the syllable containing the **-e-**. In the forms that have the stress on the ending, the **-e-** remains. Note that some are **-ar** verbs and some are **-er** verbs; the regular endings for each group should be used. Verbs ending in **-zar** and **-gar** are also spelling-change verbs: Model Verbs 6 and 7, respectively.

IMPERATIVE

(tú) piensa	(vosotros) pensad
(usted) piense	(ustedes) piensen

PLUPERFECT	**PAST ANTERIOR**
había pensado	hube pensado
FUTURE	**FUTURE PERFECT**
pensaré	habré pensado
CONDITIONAL	**CONDITIONAL PERFECT**
pensaría	habría / hubiera pensado

PRESENT SUBJUNCTIVE	**PERFECT SUBJUNCTIVE**
piense	haya pensado
pienses	
piense	
pensemos	
penséis	
piensen	

IMPERFECT SUBJUNCTIVE	**PLUPERFECT SUBJUNCTIVE**
pensara / pensase	hubiera / hubiese pensado

Cuando hace frío	**When it is cold**
Si hace frío, lo mejor es que *cierres* **la ventana. Luego,** *enciende* **el fuego en la chimenea, y** *comienza* **a llamar a tus amigos. Una vez que estén todos en tu casa,** *siéntense* **frente a la chimenea y** *empiecen* **a contar historias de terror. ¿Entendiste?**	If it is cold, the best thing to do is to *close* the window. Then, *light* a fire in the fireplace and *start* calling your friends. Once they are all at your house, *sit* in front of the fireplace and *begin* to tell scary stories. Did you understand?

type 1 stem-changing verb **o** → **ue**

GERUND	PAST PARTICIPLE
volviendo	vuelto

PRESENT INDICATIVE	PRESENT PERFECT
vuelvo	he vuelto
vuelves	
vuelve	
volvemos	
volvéis	
vuelven	

PRESENT PROGRESSIVE	IMPERFECT PROGRESSIVE
estoy volviendo	estaba volviendo

IMPERFECT INDICATIVE	PRETERITE
volvía	volví

PLUPERFECT	PAST ANTERIOR
había vuelto	hube vuelto

Similar verbs

Only a very small selection of **o** → **ue** stem-changing verbs is listed here.

acordarse	remember	**encontrar**	find, meet
costar	cost	**soler**	be accustomed / used to

Note: These verbs are type 1 stem-changing verbs and are irregular only in the present indicative and present subjunctive tenses and thus also in the imperative forms except the **vosotros** form (**volved**). The **-o-** in the stem changes to **-ue-** in forms where the stress falls on the syllable containing the **-o-**. In forms that have the stress on the ending, the **-o-** remains. Most of these verbs, are in other respects regular, but note, for example, the irregular past participle of **volver** (**vuelto**) and its compound forms, such as **envolver** (**envuelto**) and **resolver** (**resuelto**). All of these verbs are either **-ar** or **-er** verbs and take the regular endings for their group. Note, however, that verbs ending in **-car, -zar,** or **-gar** are also spelling-change verbs: ▶ Model Verbs 5, 6, and 7, respectively.

IMPERATIVE

(tú) vuelve	(vosotros) volved
(usted) vuelva	(ustedes) vuelvan

FUTURE	**FUTURE PERFECT**
volveré	habré vuelto
CONDITIONAL	**CONDITIONAL PERFECT**
volvería	habría/hubiera vuelto
PRESENT SUBJUNCTIVE	**PERFECT SUBJUNCTIVE**
vuelva	haya vuelto
vuelvas	
vuelva	
volvamos	
volváis	
vuelvan	
IMPERFECT SUBJUNCTIVE	**PLUPERFECT SUBJUNCTIVE**
volviera/volviese	hubiera/hubiese vuelto

La pesadilla

Anoche tuve un sueño extraño. Por lo general no *me acuerdo* de lo que sueño, pero esta vez fue muy sencillo *acordarse*. En el sueño, mi esposa y yo *nos encontramos* en el restaurante donde *solíamos* ir cuando éramos novios. Ella, sin embargo, no *se acordaba* del lugar. Después, me dijo que me *encontraba* extraño. Cuando *volví* la cara hacia el espejo, mis facciones eran distintas a las que *yo solía* tener. ¡Qué terrible!

The nightmare

Last night I had a weird dream. Generally, *I do* not *remember* what I dream, but this time it was easy *to remember*. In the dream, my wife and I *met* at the restaurant where *we used to* go when we were girlfriend and boyfriend. However, *she did* not *remember* the place. Then, she told me *she found* me weird. When *I turned* my face to the mirror, my features were different from the ones *I used to* have. How terrible!

21 jugar   play; gamble

type 1 stem-changing verb **u** → **ue**

GERUND	PAST PARTICIPLE
jugando	jugado

PRESENT INDICATIVE	PRESENT PERFECT
juego	he jugado
juegas	
juega	
jugamos	
jugáis	
juegan	

PRESENT PROGRESSIVE	IMPERFECT PROGRESSIVE
estoy jugando	estaba jugando

IMPERFECT INDICATIVE	PRETERITE
jugaba	jugué
jugabas	jugaste
jugaba	jugó
jugábamos	jugamos
jugábais	jugasteis
jugaban	jugaron

Note: **Jugar** is the only verb that has the **u** → **ue** spelling change. For all other purposes, it is a member of the type 1 **o** → **ue** family.

What happens with **jugar** is that the **-u-** in the stem changes to **-ue-** in those forms in which the stress falls on the syllable containing **-u-**. In those forms that have the stress on the ending, the **-u-** remains. Since it is only in the present and present subjunctive tenses where some forms have the stress on the stem, this change does not occur in the other tenses.

Note, however, the **u** in the first person singular of the preterite tense and in all the forms of the present subjunctive tense. This is simply to preserve the pronunciation of the hard **g** in those forms where the verb ending begins with an **e**.

IMPERATIVE	
(tú) juega	(vosotros) jugad
(usted) juegue	(ustedes) jueguen

PLUPERFECT	PAST ANTERIOR
había jugado	hube jugado

FUTURE	FUTURE PERFECT
jugaré	habré jugado

CONDITIONAL	CONDITIONAL PERFECT
jugaría	habría/hubiera jugado

PRESENT SUBJUNCTIVE

PERFECT SUBJUNCTIVE

juegue   haya jugado
juegues
juegue
juguemos
juguéis
jueguen

IMPERFECT SUBJUNCTIVE	PLUPERFECT SUBJUNCTIVE
jugara/jugase	hubiera/hubiese jugado

Pepe *juega* otra vez por la selección argentina.	Pepe *plays* again for the Argentinian team.
Los niños que *juegan* en la calle corren grandes riesgos.	Children who *play* in the street run great risks.
No *juegues* todo tu dinero.	*Don't gamble* all your money away.
Si yo fuera más alto, *jugaría* baloncesto.	If I were taller, *I would play* basketball.

type 2 stem-changing verb **e** → **ie** and **i**

GERUND	PAST PARTICIPLE
sintiendo	sentido

PRESENT INDICATIVE	PRESENT PERFECT
siento	he sentido
sientes	
siente	
sentimos	
sentís	
sienten	

PRESENT PROGRESSIVE	IMPERFECT PROGRESSIVE
estoy sintiendo	estaba sintiendo

IMPERFECT INDICATIVE	PRETERITE
sentía	sentí
	sentiste
	sintió
	sentimos
	sentisteis
	sintieron

Similar verbs

advertir	warn, advise	**mentir**	lie
diferir	differ	**preferir**	prefer
divertirse	enjoy oneself	**referir**	refer, relate
herir	wound, hurt	**sugerir**	suggest

Note: These verbs are type 2 stem-changing verbs and are all **-ir** verbs. They have the change **e** → **ie** in some forms of the present indicative and present subjunctive tenses, and therefore also in the imperative forms except the **vosotros** form (**sentid**). What happens is that the **-e-** in the stem changes to **-ie-** in those forms in which the stress falls on the syllable containing the **-e-**. In those forms that have the stress on the ending, the **-e-** remains. In addition, these verbs have a change from **e** → **i** in the gerund, in the first and second persons plural forms of the present tense, in the third person forms of the preterite tense, and in all forms of the imperfect subjunctive tense. These verbs are regular in other respects.

IMPERATIVE
(tú) siente

(usted) sienta

(vosotros) sentid

(ustedes) sientan

PLUPERFECT
había sentido

PAST ANTERIOR
hube sentido

FUTURE
sentiré

FUTURE PERFECT
habré sentido

CONDITIONAL
sentiría

CONDITIONAL PERFECT
habría/hubiera sentido

PRESENT SUBJUNCTIVE
sienta

sientas

sienta

sintamos

sintáis

sientan

PERFECT SUBJUNCTIVE
haya sentido

IMPERFECT SUBJUNCTIVE
sintiera/sintiese

PLUPERFECT SUBJUNCTIVE
hubiera/hubiese sentido

Un consejo

Está bien que *te diviertas*, pero te *advierto* que es malo pasar todo el tiempo jugando. Te *sugiero* que estudies con tu amiga; si *prefieren*, pueden hacerlo en su casa. Pero por favor no me *mientan*, porque eso *hiere* mis sentimientos.

Some advice

It is fine for *you to have a good time*, but *I warn* you that it is not good to spend all your time playing. *I suggest* that you study with your friend; if *you both prefer*, you can do so at her house. But please *do* not *lie* to me, because that *hurts* my feelings.

23 dormir(se)   sleep; fall asleep

type 2 stem-changing verb **o** → **ue** and **u**

GERUND	PAST PARTICIPLE
durmiendo	dormido

PRESENT INDICATIVE	PRESENT PERFECT
duermo	he dormido
duermes	
duerme	
dormimos	
dormís	
duermen	

PRESENT PROGRESSIVE	IMPERFECT PROGRESSIVE
estoy durmiendo	estaba durmiendo

IMPERFECT INDICATIVE	PRETERITE
dormía	dormí
	dormiste
	durmió
	dormimos
	dormisteis
	durmieron

Similar verb

morir   die

Note: These verbs are type 2 stem-changing verbs. They change from **o** → **ue** in the present indicative and present subjunctive tenses, and therefore also in the imperative forms except the **vosotros** form (**dormid**). What happens is that the **-o-** in the stem changes to **-ue-** in those forms in which the stress falls on the syllable containing the **-o-**. In those forms that have the stress on the ending, the **-o-** remains. In addition, these two verbs change from **o** → **u** in the gerund, in the third person forms of the preterite tense, in all forms of the imperfect subjunctive forms, and in the first and second persons plural forms of the present subjunctive tense. All of these forms, have an ending beginning with an **-i-**. These verbs are regular in other respects, but note the irregular past participle of **morir** (**muerto**).

IMPERATIVE

(tú) duerme

(usted) duerma

(vosotros) dormid

(ustedes) duerman

PLUPERFECT

había dormido

PAST ANTERIOR

hube dormido

FUTURE

dormiré

FUTURE PERFECT

habré dormido

CONDITIONAL

dormiría

CONDITIONAL PERFECT

habría/hubiera dormido

PRESENT SUBJUNCTIVE

duerma

duermas

duerma

durmamos

durmáis

duerman

PERFECT SUBJUNCTIVE

haya dormido

IMPERFECT SUBJUNCTIVE

durmiera/durmiese

PLUPERFECT SUBJUNCTIVE

hubiera/hubiese dormido

Las noticias

The news

CINCO PERSONAS *MURIERON* EN UN ACCIDENTE DE TRÁNSITO

FIVE PERSONS *DIED* IN A CAR ACCIDENT

CHOFER *SE DURMIÓ:* ES UN MILAGRO QUE NADIE *HAYA MUERTO*

DRIVER *FELL ASLEEP:* IT IS A MIRACLE THAT NOBODY *HAS DIED*

HACE UNA SEMANA QUE EL PRESIDENTE NO *DUERME*

IT'S BEEN A WEEK THAT THE PRESIDENT *HASN'T SLEPT*

ENFERMO *MORIRÁ* SI NO CONSIGUE UN DONANTE DE RIÑÓN

SICK MAN *WILL DIE* IF HE DOESN'T GET A KIDNEY DONOR

24 pedir   request, ask for; order

type 3 stem-changing verb **e** → **i**

GERUND	PAST PARTICIPLE
pidiendo	pedido

PRESENT INDICATIVE	PRESENT PERFECT
pido	he pedido
pides	
pide	
pedimos	
pedís	
piden	

PRESENT PROGRESSIVE	IMPERFECT PROGRESSIVE
estoy pidiendo	estaba pidiendo

IMPERFECT INDICATIVE	PRETERITE
pedía	pedí
	pediste
	pidió
	pedimos
	pedisteis
	pidieron

Similar verbs

conseguir	manage, get hold of	**reñir**	scold
corregir	correct	**repetir**	repeat
despedir(se)	fire, dismiss; say good-bye to, take leave of	**seguir**	follow, carry on
elegir	elect, choose	**servir**	serve
gemir	groan	**sonreír**	smile
impedir	prevent	**teñir**	dye
regir	rule	**vestir(se)**	dress
reírse	laugh		

(plus any compounds of these verbs)

Note: These verbs, which are all **-ir** verbs, are type 3 stem-changing verbs. Their stems have the spelling change **e** → **i** in most forms of the present indicative tense and in all forms of the present subjunctive tense, and therefore in the imperative forms except for the **vosotros** form (**pedid**). It also occurs in the third person forms of the preterite tense and in all forms of the imperfect subjunctive tense, and in the gerund.

STEM-CHANGING VERBS **pedir** 24

IMPERATIVE
(tú) pide
(usted) pida

(vosotros) pedid
(ustedes) pidan

PLUPERFECT
había pedido

PAST ANTERIOR
hube pedido

FUTURE
pediré

FUTURE PERFECT
habré pedido

CONDITIONAL
pediría

CONDITIONAL PERFECT
habría/hubiera pedido

PRESENT SUBJUNCTIVE
pida
pidas
pida
pidamos
pidáis
pidan

PERFECT SUBJUNCTIVE
haya pedido

IMPERFECT SUBJUNCTIVE
pidiera/pidiese

PLUPERFECT SUBJUNCTIVE
hubiera/hubiese pedido

Pide lo que quieras.

Order whatever you want.

Si me *despidieran*, no podría pagar el alquiler.

If *they fired* me, I wouldn't be able to pay the rent.

Estaban sirviendo la cena cuando sonó la alarma.

They were serving dinner when the alarm went off.

Pediré una bicicleta nueva para Navidad.

I will ask for a new bicycle for Christmas.

No te *habría despedido* si no fueras tan flojo.

*I would*n't *have fired* you if you were not so lazy.

93

Irregular Verbs

The following are the most common irregular verbs in Spanish. Some of them have a unique spelling change, while others do not conform to a predictable pattern.

In the future and conditional tenses, only the stem can be irregular; the set of endings is always the same. Therefore, only the first person singular form is given. For the full set of endings, see The Complete System of Tenses in Spanish [Model Verb 1]. Any irregularity in the future tense stem will apply to the conditional as well.

Except for **ser** and **ir,** the imperfect indicative and subjunctive tenses of all verbs are regular, and either the **-ar** or **-er/-ir** set of endings must be used. Therefore, only the first person singular form is given; the others are easy to work out from the Regular Verbs [Model Verbs 2, 3, 4].

Similarly, compound tenses using the auxiliaries **estar** or **haber** are not given in full: for the whole set of forms, consult the tables for **estar** or **haber** [Model Verbs 38, 40] or look at The Complete System of Tenses in Spanish [Model Verb 1].

Verbs with a **pretérito grave** [The Verb System in Spanish, 10b(ix)] are marked **(pg)**.

Verbs with present indicative and subjunctive forms that follow the stem-change pattern described in The Verb System in Spanish, 10b(v) [Model Verbs 19–24], are marked **(sc)**.

GERUND	PAST PARTICIPLE
abriendo	abierto

PRESENT INDICATIVE	PRESENT PERFECT
abro	he abierto
abres	
abre	
abrimos	
abrís	
abren	

PRESENT PROGRESSIVE	IMPERFECT PROGRESSIVE
estoy abriendo	estaba abriendo

IMPERFECT INDICATIVE	PRETERITE
abría	abrí
	abriste
	abrió
	abrimos
	abristeis
	abrieron

Similar verbs

cubrir	cover	**entreabrir**	half open
descubrir	discover, uncover		

Note: The only irregularity lies in the formation of the past participle. In every other respect, these are regular verbs of the **-ir** family.

IMPERATIVE

(tú) abre   (vosotros) abrid
(usted) abra   (ustedes) abran

PLUPERFECT   *PAST ANTERIOR*
había/abierto   hube/abierto

FUTURE   *FUTURE PERFECT*
abriré   habré abierto

CONDITIONAL   *CONDITIONAL PERFECT*
abriría   habría/hubiera abierto

PRESENT SUBJUNCTIVE   *PERFECT SUBJUNCTIVE*
abra   haya abierto
abras
abra
abramos
abráis
abran

IMPERFECT SUBJUNCTIVE   *PLUPERFECT SUBJUNCTIVE*
abriera/abriese   hubiera/hubiese abierto

Unos avisos   **A few notices**

ABIERTO DE 9 A 5   *OPEN* FROM 9 TO 5

ABRA EL GRIFO CON CUIDADO   *TURN* THE FAUCET ON WITH CARE

**ESTA PUERTA SE ABRE CON TARJETA   THIS DOOR *OPENS* WITH AN
ELECTRÓNICA SOLAMENTE**   ELECTRONIC CARD ONLY

ABRIMOS EL 1° DE SEPTIEMBRE   *WE OPEN* ON SEPTEMBER 1ST

**ESTA TIENDA NO ABRIRÁ EL PRÓXIMO THIS STORE *WILL* NOT *OPEN* NEXT
DOMINGO**   SUNDAY

(sc)

GERUND	PAST PARTICIPLE
adquiriendo	adquirido

PRESENT INDICATIVE	PRESENT PERFECT
adquiero	he adquirido
adquieres	
adquiere	
adquirimos	
adquirís	
adquieren	

PRESENT PROGRESSIVE	IMPERFECT PROGRESSIVE
estoy adquiriendo	estaba adquiriendo

IMPERFECT INDICATIVE	PRETERITE
adquiría	adquirí
	adquiriste
	adquirió
	adquirimos
	adquiristeis
	adquirieron

Note: This verb behaves like a stem-changing verb when the stem vowel is stressed; elsewhere, the **-i-** of the infinitive stem remains.

IMPERATIVE
(tú) adquiere
(usted) adquiera

(vosotros) adquirid
(ustedes) adquieran

PLUPERFECT
había adquirido

PAST ANTERIOR
hube adquirido

FUTURE
adquiriré

FUTURE PERFECT
habré adquirido

CONDITIONAL
adquiriría

CONDITIONAL PERFECT
habría / hubiera adquirido

PRESENT SUBJUNCTIVE
adquiera
adquieras
adquiera
adquiramos
adquiráis
adquieran

PERFECT SUBJUNCTIVE
haya adquirido

IMPERFECT SUBJUNCTIVE
adquiriera / adquiriese

PLUPERFECT SUBJUNCTIVE
hubiera / hubiese adquirido

Habíamos adquirido un auto nuevo, pero tuvimos que devolverlo.

We had purchased a new car, but we had to return it.

Está adquiriendo un departamento a plazos.

He is purchasing an apartment in installments.

Adquirí una gran experiencia gracias a mis viajes por todo el mundo.

I acquired a lot of experience thanks to my trips all around the world.

(pg)

GERUND	PAST PARTICIPLE
andando	andado

PRESENT INDICATIVE	PRESENT PERFECT
ando	he andado
andas	
anda	
andamos	
andáis	
andan	

PRESENT PROGRESSIVE	IMPERFECT PROGRESSIVE
estoy andando	estaba andando

IMPERFECT INDICATIVE	PRETERITE
andaba	anduve
	anduviste
	anduvo
	anduvimos
	anduvisteis
	anduvieron

Note: The preterite forms and consequently the imperfect subjunctive forms (of **pretérito grave** type) are the only irregularities. In every other respect, **andar** behaves like a regular **-ar** verb.

IMPERATIVE
(tú) anda   (vosotros) andad
(usted) ande   (ustedes) anden

PLUPERFECT   *PAST ANTERIOR*
había andado   hube andado

FUTURE   *FUTURE PERFECT*
andaré   habré andado

CONDITIONAL   *CONDITIONAL PERFECT*
andaría   habría/hubiera andado

PRESENT SUBJUNCTIVE   *PERFECT SUBJUNCTIVE*
ande   haya andado
andes
ande
andemos
andéis
anden

IMPERFECT SUBJUNCTIVE   *PLUPERFECT SUBJUNCTIVE*
anduviera/anduviese   hubiera/hubiese andado

Dime con quién *andas* y te diré quién eres.	Tell me who *you go around* with and I'll tell you who you are.
***Andamos* muchas horas antes de encontrar una farmacia.**	*We walked* for many hours before finding a drugstore.
Siempre voy *andando* al colegio.	*I* always *walk* to school.
Si no *anduviera* tanto, mi padre estaría muy gordo.	If *he* did*n't walk* so much, my father would be very fat.

28 bendecir   bless

(sc + pg)

GERUND	PAST PARTICIPLE
bendiciendo	bendecido

PRESENT INDICATIVE	PRESENT PERFECT
bendigo	he bendecido
bendices	
bendice	
bendecimos	
bendecís	
bendicen	

PRESENT PROGRESSIVE	IMPERFECT PROGRESSIVE
estoy bendiciendo	estaba bendiciendo

IMPERFECT INDICATIVE	PRETERITE
bendecía	bendije
	bendijiste
	bendijo
	bendijimos
	bendijisteis
	bendijeron

PLUPERFECT	PAST ANTERIOR
había bendecido	hube bendecido

Similar verb

maldecir   curse, damn

Note: The key irregularities are:

- the first person singular form of the present tense, and therefore all of the present subjunctive forms take **-g-** in place of **-c-;**
- the present indicative tense, which behaves like a type 3 stem-changing verb;
- the **pretérito grave** and therefore the imperfect subjunctive forms.

In other respects, **bendecir** behaves like a regular **-ir** verb. It largely follows its 'parent' verb, **decir**, with the following exceptions:

- the past participle, which is regular, unlike **decir** (**dicho**);
- the singular familiar imperative, which is regular (unlike **di**);
- the regular formation of the future and conditional stem.

IMPERATIVE
(tú) bendice
(usted) bendiga

(vosotros) bendecid
(ustedes) bendigan

FUTURE
bendeciré
bendecirás
bendecirá
bendeciremos
bendeciréis
bendecirán

FUTURE PERFECT
habré bendecido

CONDITIONAL
bendeciría

CONDITIONAL PERFECT
habría/hubiera bendecido

PRESENT SUBJUNCTIVE
bendiga
bendigas
bendiga
bendigamos
bendigáis
bendigan

PERFECT SUBJUNCTIVE
haya bendecido

IMPERFECT SUBJUNCTIVE
bendijera/bendijese

PLUPERFECT SUBJUNCTIVE
hubiera/hubiese bendecido

¡*Bendígame*, Padre, pues he pecado!

Bless me, Father, for I have sinned!

¡Dios te *bendiga!*

May God *bless* you!

El Papa *bendecirá* la nueva catedral.

The Pope *will bless* the new cathedral.

La gente *maldijo* a los soldados que atacaron el templo.

The people *damned* the soldiers who attacked the temple.

(pg)

GERUND	PAST PARTICIPLE
cabiendo	cabido

PRESENT INDICATIVE	PRESENT PERFECT
quepo	he cabido
cabes	
cabe	
cabemos	
cabéis	
caben	

PRESENT PROGRESSIVE	IMPERFECT PROGRESSIVE
estoy cabiendo	estaba cabiendo

IMPERFECT INDICATIVE	PRETERITE
cabía	cupe
	cupiste
	cupo
	cupimos
	cupisteis
	cupieron

Note: The key irregularities are:

- the first person singular form of the present tense, and therefore the present subjunctive tense;
- the **pretérito grave** and therefore the imperfect subjunctive tense;
- the future tense stem.

IMPERATIVE	
(tú) cabe	(vosotros) cabed
(usted) quepa	(ustedes) quepan

PLUPERFECT	*PAST ANTERIOR*
había cabido	hube cabido
FUTURE	*FUTURE PERFECT*
cabré	habré cabido
CONDITIONAL	*CONDITIONAL PERFECT*
cabría	habría/hubiera cabido
PRESENT SUBJUNCTIVE	*PERFECT SUBJUNCTIVE*
quepa	haya cabido
quepas	
quepa	
quepamos	
quepáis	
quepan	
IMPERFECT SUBJUNCTIVE	*PLUPERFECT SUBJUNCTIVE*
cupiera/cupiese	hubiera/hubiese cabido

¡El auto es muy pequeño, no *cabremos* todos!	The car is very small, *we will* not all *fit*!
Si quieres que *quepan* todos los muebles, debemos ampliar la casa.	If you want all the furniture *to fit*, we must expand the house.

GERUND	PAST PARTICIPLE
cayendo	caído

PRESENT INDICATIVE	PRESENT PERFECT
caigo	he caído
caes	
cae	
caemos	
caéis	
caen	

PRESENT PROGRESSIVE	IMPERFECT PROGRESSIVE
estoy cayendo	estaba cayendo

IMPERFECT INDICATIVE	PRETERITE
caía	caí
	caíste
	cayó
	caímos
	caísteis
	cayeron

Similar verb

decaer   decay, decline

Note: The key irregularities are:

• the first person singular form of the present indicative tense and so all forms of the present subjunctive tense are based on the stem **caig-**;
• a **-y-** is needed in the third person forms of the preterite tense;
• an accent is needed on the **-i-** when it is stressed.

The verbs **roer** (gnaw) and **corroer** (corrode) follow a largely similar pattern.

IMPERATIVE

(tú) cae

(usted) caiga

(vosotros) caed

(ustedes) caigan

PLUPERFECT

había caído

PAST ANTERIOR

hube caído

FUTURE

caeré

FUTURE PERFECT

habré caido

CONDITIONAL

caería

CONDITIONAL PERFECT

habría/hubiera caído

PRESENT SUBJUNCTIVE

caiga

caigas

caiga

caigamos

caigáis

caigan

PLUPERFECT SUBJUNCTIVE

haya caído

IMPERFECT SUBJUNCTIVE

cayera/cayese

PLUPERFECT SUBJUNCTIVE

hubiera/hubiese caído

¡Ten cuidado, o *te caerás*!

Se cayó en un hoyo enorme.

¡*Caed* de rodillas!

Be careful or *you will fall*!

He fell into a huge hole.

Fall on your knees!

31 conducir   drive; lead; conduct

(pg)

GERUND	PAST PARTICIPLE
conduciendo	conducido

PRESENT INDICATIVE	PRESENT PERFECT
conduzco	he conducido
conduces	
conduce	
conducimos	
conducís	
conducen	

PRESENT PROGRESSIVE	IMPERFECT PROGRESSIVE
estoy conduciendo	estaba conduciendo

IMPERFECT INDICATIVE	PRETERITE
conducía	conduje
	condujiste
	condujo
	condujimos
	condujisteis
	condujeron

Similar verbs

All verbs ending in **-ducir**:

aducir	adduce	**producir**	produce, generate, yield
deducir	deduce	**reducir**	lower, reduce, shorten
inducir	induce	**reproducir**	reproduce
introducir	introduce, bring in, insert	**traducir**	translate

Note: The key irregularities are:

- the first person singular form of the present tense, and therefore all of the present subjunctive forms take **-zc-** in place of **-c-;**
- the **pretérito grave** and therefore the imperfect subjunctive tense.

IMPERATIVE
(tú) conduce
(usted) conduzca

(vosotros) conducid
(ustedes) conduzcan

PLUPERFECT
había conducido

PAST ANTERIOR
hube conducido

FUTURE
conduciré

FUTURE PERFECT
habré conducido

CONDITIONAL
conduciría

CONDITIONAL PERFECT
habría/hubiera conducido

PRESENT SUBJUNCTIVE
conduzca
conduzcas
conduzca
conduzcamos
conduzcáis
conduzcan

PERFECT SUBJUNCTIVE
haya conducido

IMPERFECT SUBJUNCTIVE
condujera/condujese

PLUPERFECT SUBJUNCTIVE
hubiera/hubiese conducido

El profesor *tradujo* la carta.	The teacher *translated* the letter.
***Introduzca* una moneda.**	*Insert* a coin.
El chofer *conducía* muy de prisa.	The driver *drove* very fast.
Si no me lo decías, lo *hubiera deducido* de todos modos.	If you didn't tell me, *I would have deduced* it anyway.

32 conocer   know; get to know; meet

GERUND	PAST PARTICIPLE
conociendo	conocido

PRESENT INDICATIVE	PRESENT PERFECT
conozco	he conocido
conoces	
conoce	
conocemos	
conocéis	
conocen	

PRESENT PROGRESSIVE	IMPERFECT PROGRESSIVE
estoy conociendo	estaba conociendo

IMPERFECT INDICATIVE	PRETERITE
conocía	conocí
	conociste
	conoció
	conocimos
	conocisteis
	conocieron

Similar verbs

abastecer	provide, supply	**embellecer**	embellish, beautify
aborrecer	hate, abhor	**encanecer**	go gray
acontecer	happen, occur	**endurecer(se)**	harden
agradecer	thank	**enfurecer**	enrage, madden
amanecer	dawn	**enloquecer**	madden
anochecer	get dark	**enriquecer(se)**	enrich
aparecer	appear	**ensordecer**	deafen
apetecer	feel like, want	**entristecer**	sadden
carecer	lack	**envejecer**	age
compadecer	pity, sympathize	**envilecer**	degrade
crecer	grow	**esclarecer**	clear up
desaparecer	disappear	**establecer**	establish, set up
desconocer	not know	**estremecerse**	quiver, shiver
desobedecer	disobey	**favorecer**	favor

IMPERATIVE	
(tú) conoce	(vosotros) conoced
(usted) conozca	(ustedes) conozcan

PLUPERFECT	*PAST ANTERIOR*
había conocido	hube conocido
FUTURE	*FUTURE PERFECT*
conoceré	habré conocido
CONDITIONAL	*CONDITIONAL PERFECT*
conocería	habría/hubiera conocido
PRESENT SUBJUNCTIVE	*PERFECT SUBJUNCTIVE*
conozca	haya conocido
conozcas	
conozca	
conozcamos	
conozcáis	
conozcan	
IMPERFECT SUBJUNCTIVE	*PLUPERFECT SUBJUNCTIVE*
conociera/conociese	hubiera/hubiese conocido

---

florecer	flourish, flower, bloom	**oscurecer**	grow dark
fortalecer	strengthen	**padecer**	suffer
humedecer	dampen, moisten	**palidecer**	turn pale
languidecer	languish, pine (away)	**parecer**	appear, seem
merecer	deserve	**pertenecer**	belong
nacer	be born	**reconocer**	acknowledge, recognize

Note: The only irregularities are the first person singular form of the present indicative tense, and in consequence all forms of the present subjunctive tense.

Nos conocimos en Madrid.	*We met* in Madrid.
Los niños crecen rápidamente.	Children *grow* quickly.
El hombre desapareció al final de la calle.	The man *disappeared* at the end of the street.

GERUND	***PAST PARTICIPLE***
dando	dado

PRESENT INDICATIVE	***PRESENT PERFECT***
doy	he dado
das	
da	
damos	
dais	
dan	

PRESENT PROGRESSIVE	***IMPERFECT PROGRESSIVE***
estoy dando	estaba dando

IMPERFECT INDICATIVE	***PRETERITE***
daba	di
	diste
	dio
	dimos
	disteis
	dieron

Note: The key irregularities are:

- the first person singular form of the present tense, ending in **-oy;**
- the accent on the form **dé,** needed to distinguish it from the preposition **de;**
- the preterite forms, in which **dar** behaves like an **-er/-ir** verb, and needs no written accents;
- the imperfect subjunctive forms, based on the preterite stem.

IMPERATIVE
(tú) da   (vosotros) dad
(usted) dé   (ustedes) den

PLUPERFECT   *PAST ANTERIOR*
había dado   hube dado

FUTURE   *FUTURE PERFECT*
daré   habré dado

CONDITIONAL   *CONDITIONAL PERFECT*
daría   habría/hubiera dado

PRESENT SUBJUNCTIVE   *PERFECT SUBJUNCTIVE*
dé   haya dado
des
dé
demos
deis
den

IMPERFECT SUBJUNCTIVE   *PLUPERFECT SUBJUNCTIVE*
diera/diese   hubiera/hubiese dado

Mi padre me *dio* sólo cien pesos.

My father *gave* me only a hundred pesos.

***Dame* todo lo que tienes.**

Give me everything you have.

***Hubiera dado* todo lo que tengo por conocerte antes.**

I'd have given everything I have to have met you before.

El gobierno *dará* alimentos a las personas desempleadas.

The government *will give* food to unemployed people.

34 decir   say; tell

(sc + pg)

GERUND	PAST PARTICIPLE
diciendo	dicho

PRESENT INDICATIVE	PRESENT PERFECT
digo	he dicho
dices	
dice	
decimos	
decís	
dicen	

PRESENT PROGRESSIVE	IMPERFECT PROGRESSIVE
estoy diciendo	estaba diciendo

IMPERFECT INDICATIVE	PRETERITE
decía	dije
	dijiste
	dijo
	dijimos
	dijisteis
	dijeron

Similar verbs

contradecir(se)	contradict (oneself)	**predecir**	predict
desdecir(se)	clash with, withdraw		

Note: The key irregularities are:

• the first person singular form of the present tense, and therefore all forms of the present subjunctive tense, take **-g-** in place of **-c-;**
• the present indicative tense, which behaves like a type 3 stem-changing verb;
• the **pretérito grave,** and therefore the imperfect subjunctive forms;
• the past participle forms, similar to those of **hacer** (**hecho**);
• the future and conditional stem, **dir-.**

IMPERATIVE

(tú) di	(vosotros) decid
(usted) diga	(ustedes) digan

PLUPERFECT	**PAST ANTERIOR**
había dicho	hube dicho
FUTURE	**FUTURE PERFECT**
diré	habré dicho
CONDITIONAL	**CONDITIONAL PERFECT**
diría	habría/hubiera dicho
PRESENT SUBJUNCTIVE	**PERFECT SUBJUNCTIVE**
diga	haya dicho
digas	
diga	
digamos	
digáis	
digan	
IMPERFECT SUBJUNCTIVE	**PLUPERFECT SUBJUNCTIVE**
dijera/dijese	hubiera/hubiese dicho

¡*Dicho* y hecho!	No sooner *said* than done!
¡*Dicen* que es loco!	*They say* he's crazy!
***Digan* lo que *digan*...**	Whatever *they say* . . .
El adivino no *predijo* lo que le iba a pasar.	The fortune-teller *did*n't *predict* what was going to happen to him.
***Estoy diciendo* todo lo que sé.**	*I am telling* everything I know.
No te *contradigas*.	*Do* not *contradict* yourself.
El ministro *se desdijo* de sus anteriores declaraciones.	The minister *withdrew* his previous statements.

35 erguir(se)   raise; lift; straighten up

GERUND	PAST PARTICIPLE
irguiendo	erguido

PRESENT INDICATIVE	PRESENT PERFECT
yergo/irgo	he erguido
yergues/irgues	
yergue/irgue	
erguimos	
erguís	
yerguen/irguen	

PRESENT PROGRESSIVE	IMPERFECT PROGRESSIVE
estoy irguiendo	estaba irguiendo

IMPERFECT INDICATIVE	PRETERITE
erguía	erguí
	erguiste
	irguió
	erguimos
	erguisteis
	irguieron

Note: This verb has three possible stems, and in some forms two alternative forms exist. The **ye-** stem is basically due to this verb being a stem-changing verb: instead of beginning with **ie-**, however, stressed-stem forms begin with **ye-**. Note the **-u-** needed in all forms in which the verb ending begins with an **-e**. The one regular feature of this verb is that all its endings follow the pattern for a regular **-ir** verb [**vivir** 4].

IMPERATIVE
(tú) yergue/irgue
(usted) yerga/irga

(vosotros) erguid
(ustedes) yergan/irgan

PLUPERFECT
había erguido

PAST ANTERIOR
hube erguido

FUTURE
erguiré

FUTURE PERFECT
habré erguido

CONDITIONAL
erguiría

CONDITIONAL PERFECT
habría/hubiera erguido

PRESENT SUBJUNCTIVE
yerga/irga
yergas/irgas
yerga/irga
yergamos/irgamos
yergáis/irgáis
yergan/irgan

PERFECT SUBJUNCTIVE
haya erguido

IMPERFECT SUBJUNCTIVE
irguiera/irguiese

PLUPERFECT SUBJUNCTIVE
hubiera/hubiese erguido

¡Ponte *erguido!*

La torre *se yergue* sobre la ciudad.

Los soldados *se irguieron* cuando entró el general.

Straighten up!

The tower *rises* over the city.

The soldiers *straightened up* when the general came in.

(sc)

GERUND	PAST PARTICIPLE
errando	errado

PRESENT INDICATIVE	PRESENT PERFECT
yerro	he errado
yerras	
yerra	
erramos	
erráis	
yerran	

PRESENT PROGRESSIVE	IMPERFECT PROGRESSIVE
estoy errando	estaba errando

IMPERFECT INDICATIVE	PRETERITE
erraba	erré
	erraste
	erró
	erramos
	errasteis
	erraron

Note: This verb is basically a stem-changing **-ar** verb. However, the stressed-stem forms begin with **ye-,** rather than with **ie-**. In forms where the stem is unstressed, the **err-** remains. All endings are those of a regular **-ar** verb.

IMPERATIVE
(tú) yerra
(usted) yerre

(vosotros) errad
(ustedes) yerren

PLUPERFECT	*PAST ANTERIOR*
había errado	hube errado
FUTURE	*FUTURE PERFECT*
erraré	habré errado
CONDITIONAL	*CONDITIONAL PERFECT*
erraría	habría/hubiera errado

PRESENT SUBJUNCTIVE
yerre
yerres
yerre
erremos
erréis
yerren

PERFECT SUBJUNCTIVE
haya errado

IMPERFECT SUBJUNCTIVE
errara/errase

PLUPERFECT SUBJUNCTIVE
hubiera/hubiese errado

Estamos errando por lugares inexplorados.

We are wandering by unexplored sites.

Erré muchas veces antes de acertar.

I erred many times before scoring.

GERUND	PAST PARTICIPLE
escribiendo	escrito

PRESENT INDICATIVE	PRESENT PERFECT
escribo	he escrito
escribes	
escribe	
escribimos	
escribís	
escriben	

PRESENT PROGRESSIVE	IMPERFECT PROGRESSIVE
estoy escribiendo	estaba escribiendo

IMPERFECT INDICATIVE	PRETERITE
escribía	escribí
	escribiste
	escribió
	escribimos
	escribiste
	escribieron

Similar verbs

describir	describe	**suscribir**	subscribe
inscribir	inscribe, enroll	**transcribir**	transcribe
proscribir	proscribe		

Note: The only irregularity of this verb is its past participle, **escrito**.

IMPERATIVE
(tú) escribe
(usted) escriba

(vosotros) escribid
(ustedes) escriban

PLUPERFECT
había escrito

PAST ANTERIOR
hube escrito

FUTURE
escribiré

FUTURE PERFECT
habré escrito

CONDITIONAL
escribiría

CONDITIONAL PERFECT
habría/hubiera escrito

PRESENT SUBJUNCTIVE
escriba
escribas
escriba
escribamos
escribáis
escriban

PERFECT SUBJUNCTIVE
haya escrito

IMPERFECT SUBJUNCTIVE
escribiera/escribiese

PLUPERFECT SUBJUNCTIVE
hubiera/hubiese escrito

¡*Escríbeme* pronto!

Write to me soon!

Nuestros amigos nos *han escrito* desde México.

Our friends *have written* to us from Mexico.

El alcalde *ha proscrito* las apuestas.

The mayor *has proscribed* gambling.

El periodista *está transcribiendo* la entrevista.

The journalist *is transcribing* the interview.

38 estar   be

(pg)

GERUND	PAST PARTICIPLE
estando	estado

PRESENT INDICATIVE	PRESENT PERFECT
estoy	he estado
estás	
está	
estamos	
estáis	
están	

PRESENT PROGRESSIVE	IMPERFECT PROGRESSIVE
(not used)	(not used)

IMPERFECT INDICATIVE	PRETERITE
estaba	estuve
	estuviste
	estuvo
	estuvimos
	estuvisteis
	estuvieron

Note: This verb looks very much like a regular **-ar** verb, and in many tenses it behaves like one. However, it has some irregular features:

• all forms of the present indicative, the present subjunctive, and the imperative tenses have the stress on the (first) vowel of the ending, and so most forms need a written accent. Note the first person singular form of the present indicative, **estoy;**
• the preterite is a typical **pretérito grave** type, and its stem is also used for the imperfect subjunctive tense.

This verb corresponds to the following uses of the verb *to be:*
• to refer to place or location;
• to refer to the state or condition of somebody or something;
• to describe a state resulting from an action or event;
• to form the present progressive and imperfect progressive tenses.

[Berlitz *Spanish Grammar Handbook* for full treatment.]

IMPERATIVE	
(tú) está/estate	(vosotros) estad
(usted) esté	(ustedes) estén

PLUPERFECT	*PAST ANTERIOR*
había estado	hube estado

FUTURE	*FUTURE PERFECT*
estaré	habré estado

CONDITIONAL	*CONDITIONAL PERFECT*
estaría	habría/hubiera estado

PRESENT SUBJUNCTIVE	*PERFECT SUBJUNCTIVE*
esté	haya estado
estés	
esté	
estemos	
estéis	
estén	

IMPERFECT SUBJUNCTIVE	*PLUPERFECT SUBJUNCTIVE*
estuviera/estuviese	hubiera/hubiese estado

¿Dónde *está* tu madre?	Where *is* your mother?
***Estuvimos* allí el año pasado.**	*We were* there last year.
***Estábamos viendo* la televisión cuando llamaste.**	*We were watching* television when you called.
Iría si no *estuviera* tan cansado.	I would go if *I were* not so tired.
El libro *estará* listo la próxima semana.	The book *will be* ready next week.

GERUND	PAST PARTICIPLE
friendo	frito

PRESENT INDICATIVE	PRESENT PERFECT
frío	he frito
fríes	
fríe	
freímos	
freís	
fríen	

PRESENT PROGRESSIVE	IMPERFECT PROGRESSIVE
estoy friendo	estaba friendo

IMPERFECT INDICATIVE	PRETERITE
freía	freí
	freíste
	frió
	freímos
	freísteis
	frieron

Note: This verb is largely a type 3 stem-changing verb, but it has the following additional irregularities:

• the accent needed whenever the -i- is stressed;
• its past participle.

IMPERATIVE

(tú) fríe   (vosotros) freíd
(usted) fría   (ustedes) frían

PLUPERFECT   **PAST ANTERIOR**
había frito   hube frito

FUTURE   **FUTURE PERFECT**
freiré   habré frito

CONDITIONAL   **CONDITIONAL PERFECT**
freiría   habría/hubiera frito

PRESENT SUBJUNCTIVE   **PERFECT SUBJUNCTIVE**
fría   haya frito
frías
fría
friamos
friais
frían

IMPERFECT SUBJUNCTIVE   **PLUPERFECT SUBJUNCTIVE**
friera/friese   hubiera/hubiese frito

Receta: pescado frito	**Recipe: fried fish**
Lava y corta el pescado en filetes. *Fríelo* en una sartén grande. Cuando lo *estés friendo*, añade sal y pimienta. No lo *frías* mucho tiempo. Después que lo *hayas frito,* cómelo de inmediato. Si *freíste* demasiado pescado, guarda el resto en la refrigeradora.	Wash the fish and cut it into fillets. *Fry it* in a large frying pan. When *you are frying* it, add salt and pepper. *Don*'t *fry* it for very long. After *you have fried* it, eat it immediately. If *you fried* too much fish, keep it in the refrigerator.

40 haber have (auxiliary)

(pg)

GERUND	PAST PARTICIPLE
habiendo	habido

PRESENT INDICATIVE
he
has
ha
hemos
habéis
han
(hay = there is/are/there)

PRESENT PERFECT*
ha habido

PRESENT PROGRESSIVE*
está habiendo

IMPERFECT PROGRESSIVE*
estaba habiendo

IMPERFECT INDICATIVE
había

PRETERITE
hube
hubiste
hubo
hubimos
hubisteis
hubieron

Note: This verb is irregular in the following respects:

• the form **hay** is used for *'there is,' 'there are'*; in other tenses the normal third person singular form is used for *'there was,' 'there were'*; etc.;
• this verb has a **pretérito grave,** with **hub-** as its stem. This is also used in the imperfect subjunctive forms;
• the future tense stem is irregular: **habr-;**
• the present subjunctive tense is very irregular, with the stem **hay-;**
• this verb is the one and only auxiliary verb used in Spanish for the following compound tenses: present perfect, pluperfect, past anterior, future perfect, conditional perfect, perfect subjunctive, and pluperfect subjunctive.

IMPERATIVE
(not used)

PLUPERFECT*
había habido

PAST ANTERIOR*
hubo habido

FUTURE
habré

FUTURE PERFECT*
habrá habido

CONDITIONAL
habría

CONDITIONAL PERFECT*
habría/hubiera habido

PRESENT SUBJUNCTIVE
haya
hayas
haya
hayamos
hayáis
hayan

PERFECT SUBJUNCTIVE*
haya habido

IMPERFECT SUBJUNCTIVE
hubiera/hubiese

PLUPERFECT SUBJUNCTIVE*
hubiera/hubiese habido

De postre, *hay* fruta fresca.

For dessert *there's* fresh fruit.

¡Vamos, de prisa, *ha habido* un accidente!

Let's go, quickly, *there has been* an accident!

Mis amigos *han llegado*.

My friends *have arrived*.

***Habíamos pagado* mil pesos.**

We had paid a thousand pesos.

* Used only in the third person singular.

41 hacer   do; make

(pg)

GERUND	PAST PARTICIPLE
haciendo	hecho

PRESENT INDICATIVE	PRESENT PERFECT
hago	he hecho
haces	
hace	
hacemos	
hacéis	
hacen	

PRESENT PROGRESSIVE	IMPERFECT PROGRESSIVE
estoy haciendo	estaba haciendo

IMPERFECT INDICATIVE	PRETERITE
hacía	hice
	hiciste
	hizo
	hicimos
	hicisteis
	hicieron

Similar verbs

contrahacer	copy, imitate	**rehacer**	redo, remake
deshacer	undo, ruin	**satisfacer**	satisfy

Note: This verb is irregular in the following respects:

• it has a **pretérito grave**, with **hic-** as its stem (but note **hizo**: the **-c-** changes to **-z-** to keep the sound the same in front of the **-o**). This stem **hic-** is also used in the imperfect subjunctive forms;
• the future tense stem is irregular: **har-**;
• the first person singular form of the present tense has the stem **hag-,** and it is used throughout the present subjunctive tense;
• the past participle is irregular (**hecho**).

IMPERATIVE	
(tú) haz	(vosotros) haced
(usted) haga	(ustedes) hagan

PLUPERFECT	*PAST ANTERIOR*
había hecho	hube hecho
FUTURE	*FUTURE PERFECT*
haré	habré hecho
CONDITIONAL	*CONDITIONAL PERFECT*
haría	habría/hubiera hecho
PRESENT SUBJUNCTIVE	*PERFECT SUBJUNCTIVE*
haga	haya hecho
hagas	
haga	
hagamos	
hagáis	
hagan	
IMPERFECT SUBJUNCTIVE	*PLUPERFECT SUBJUNCTIVE*
hiciera/hiciese	hubiera/hubiese hecho

¿*Estás satisfecho?*	*Are you satisfied?*
¿Qué *hacías* cuando te llamé anoche?	What *were you doing* when I called you last night?
¡*Hagan* sus deberes!	*Do* your homework!
Hazme un gran favor: ¡cállate!	*Do me* a big favor: Shut up!
¡Mira lo que *has hecho!*	Look at what *you have done*!
Las máquinas *están haciendo* mucho ruido.	The machines *are making* a lot of noise.

GERUND	PAST PARTICIPLE
yendo	ido

PRESENT INDICATIVE	PRESENT PERFECT
voy	he ido
vas	
va	
vamos	
vais	
van	

PRESENT PROGRESSIVE	IMPERFECT PROGRESSIVE
estoy yendo	estaba yendo

IMPERFECT INDICATIVE	PRETERITE
iba	fui
ibas	fuiste
iba	fue
íbamos	fuimos
ibais	fuisteis
iban	fueron

Note: A highly irregular verb, although its endings are often very similar to, or even the same as, most regular verbs. The first step in mastering this verb is to be able to recognize and use correctly the various different stems. The future and conditional tenses and the past participle are regular. Other major features of this verb are:

• present indicative stem **v-** with **-ar** type endings; note first person singular form (**voy**);
• present subjunctive stem **vay-**;
• irregular imperfect indicative tense, but similar to **-ar** verb pattern;
• preterite and imperfect subjunctive forms based on the stem **fu-**; both sets of forms being shared with the verb **ser**.

Note that this verb is used to form the future immediate: e.g., **Mañana vamos a ir de compras** (Tomorrow we are going to go shopping).

IMPERATIVE
(tú) ve
(usted) vaya

(vosotros) id
(ustedes) vayan

PLUPERFECT
había ido

PAST ANTERIOR
hube ido

FUTURE
iré

FUTURE PERFECT
habré ido

CONDITIONAL
iría

CONDITIONAL PERFECT
habría/hubiera ido

PRESENT SUBJUNCTIVE
vaya
vayas
vaya
vayamos
vayáis
vayan

PLUPERFECT SUBJUNCTIVE
haya ido

IMPERFECT SUBJUNCTIVE
fuera/fuese

PERFECT SUBJUNCTIVE
hubiera/hubiese ido

¡Vamos _de vacaciones_!

We're going on vacation!

Niños, mañana _vamos_ de vacaciones. La semana pasada, papá _fue a_ comprar los billetes. Ahora mismo _voy a_ hacer las maletas, y papá _va a_ llegar a casa pronto. Y ahora, chicos, _vayan a_ bañarse, y María, _vete a_ la cama ya; _vamos a_ tener que levantarnos temprano.

Children, tomorrow _we are going_ on vacation. Last week, Dad _went to_ buy the tickets. _I'm_ just _about to_ pack the suitcases, and Dad _is going to_ be home soon. Now, boys, _go_ and take a bath, and Maria, _go to_ bed now; _we are going to_ have to get up early.

GERUND	PAST PARTICIPLE
luciendo	lucido

PRESENT INDICATIVE	PRESENT PERFECT
luzco	he lucido
luces	
luce	
lucimos	
lucís	
lucen	

PRESENT PROGRESSIVE	IMPERFECT PROGRESSIVE
estoy luciendo	estaba luciendo

IMPERFECT INDICATIVE	PRETERITE
lucía	lucí
	luciste
	lució
	lucimos
	lucisteis
	lucieron

Similar verb

relucir   gleam, shine

Note: This verb and its compound **relucir** behave very much like **conducir** and its family, except that they do not have a **pretérito grave**. Thus, the first person singular form of the present indicative tense and all forms of the present subjunctive tense have the stem **luzc-**.

IMPERATIVE

(tú) luce	(vosotros) lucid
(usted) luzca	(ustedes) luzcan

PLUPERFECT
había lucido

PAST ANTERIOR
hube lucido

FUTURE
luciré

FUTURE PERFECT
habré lucido

CONDITIONAL
luciría

CONDITIONAL PERFECT
habría/hubiera lucido

PRESENT SUBJUNCTIVE
luzca
luzcas
luzca
luzcamos
luzcáis
luzcan

PERFECT SUBJUNCTIVE
haya lucido

IMPERFECT SUBJUNCTIVE
luciera/luciese

PLUPERFECT SUBJUNCTIVE
hubiera/hubiese lucido

Miles de estrellas *lucen* en el cielo de Sevilla.

Thousands of stars *shine* in the sky of Seville.

Mi amiga *lució* su vestido nuevo en la fiesta.

My friend *showed off* her new dress at the party.

Mis alumnos *se lucieron* en el concurso de matemáticas.

My students *excelled* in the math contest.

GERUND	PAST PARTICIPLE
oyendo	oído

PRESENT INDICATIVE	PRESENT PERFECT
oigo	he oído
oyes	
oye	
oímos	
oís	
oyen	

PRESENT PROGRESSIVE	IMPERFECT PROGRESSIVE
estoy oyendo	estaba oyendo

IMPERFECT INDICATIVE	PRETERITE
oía	oí
	oíste
	oyó
	oímos
	oísteis
	oyeron

Similar verb

desoír   ignore, turn a deaf ear to

Note: The key irregularities are:

• the **-i-** of the stem takes an accent when stressed (notice that it is not stressed in **oiga,** the present subjunctive, the future, or the conditional tenses);
• forms with an ending beginning with **-e-** take a **-y-** to avoid three vowels coming together;
• the first person singular form of the present indicative tense has a **-g-,** which is carried into all forms of the present subjunctive tense.

IMPERATIVE	
(tú) oye	(vosotros) oíd
(usted) oiga	(ustedes) oigan

PLUPERFECT	*PAST ANTERIOR*
había oído	hube oído

FUTURE	*FUTURE PERFECT*
oiré	habré oído

CONDITIONAL	*CONDITIONAL PERFECT*
oiría	habría / hubiera oído

PRESENT SUBJUNCTIVE	*PERFECT SUBJUNCTIVE*
oiga	haya oído
oigas	
oiga	
oigamos	
oigáis	
oigan	

IMPERFECT SUBJUNCTIVE	*PLUPERFECT SUBJUNCTIVE*
oyera / oyese	hubiera / hubiese oido

¡Habla más fuerte, no te *oigo*!	Speak up, *I* can't *hear* you!
***Oiga* usted: ¡no debe hacer eso!**	*Listen*, you musn't do that!
Si me *hubieses oído*, no tendrías este problema.	If *you had listened to* me, you wouldn't have this problem.
¿*Estás oyendo* las noticias?	*Are you listening to* the news?
No *desoigas* un buen consejo.	Don't *ignore* a good piece of advice.

GERUND	**PAST PARTICIPLE**
oliendo	olido

PRESENT INDICATIVE	**PRESENT PERFECT**
huelo	he olido
hueles	
huele	
olemos	
oléis	
huelen	

PRESENT PROGRESSIVE	**IMPERFECT PROGRESSIVE**
estoy oliendo	estaba oliendo

IMPERFECT INDICATIVE	**PRETERITE**
olía	olí
	oliste
	olió
	olimos
	olisteis
	olieron

Note: **Oler** is a predictable type 1 stem-changing verb with a particular oddity: the **o-** changes to **-ue-** when the stem is stressed, but the **-ue-** is always preceded by **h-;** then, forms in which the stem is stressed begin with **hue-**. In other respects it is a normal stem-changing verb.

IMPERATIVE
(tú) huele
(usted) huela

(vosotros) oled
(ustedes) huelan

PLUPERFECT
había olido

PAST ANTERIOR
hube olido

FUTURE
oleré

FUTURE PERFECT
habré olido

CONDITIONAL
olería

CONDITIONAL PERFECT
habría/hubiera olido

PRESENT SUBJUNCTIVE
huela
huelas
huela
olamos
oláis
huelan

PERFECT SUBJUNCTIVE
haya olido

IMPERFECT SUBJUNCTIVE
oliera/oliese

PLUPERFECT SUBJUNCTIVE
hubiera/hubiese olido

Este pastel *huele* a quemado.

This cake *smells* burnt.

¡Qué bien *huelen* estas manzanas!

These apples *smell* so good!

La habitación *olía* a jazmín.

The room *smelled* of jasmine.

De repente, los perros *olieron* el zorro.

Suddenly, the dogs *smelled* the fox.

Muchachos, ¡*huelan* esto! Parece estar podrido.

Boys, *smell* this! It seems to be rotten.

46 poder   be able to; can; may

(pg)

GERUND	PAST PARTICIPLE
pudiendo	podido

PRESENT INDICATIVE	PRESENT PERFECT
puedo	he podido
puedes	
puede	
podemos	
podéis	
pueden	

PRESENT PROGRESSIVE	IMPERFECT PROGRESSIVE
estoy pudiendo	estaba pudiendo

IMPERFECT INDICATIVE	PRETERITE
podía	pude
	pudiste
	pudo
	pudimos
	pudisteis
	pudieron

Note: This verb has the following irregularities:

• the stem changes in the present indicative and subjunctive tenses are those of a type 1 **o → e** stem-changing verb;
• this is a **pretérito grave** verb, with the stem **pud-,** which is carried over into the imperfect subjunctive forms:
• in addition, the gerund is **pudiendo**;
• the future and conditional stem loses the **-e-** of the infinitive, becoming **podr-**.

IMPERATIVE
(not used)

PLUPERFECT
había podido

PAST ANTERIOR
hube podido

FUTURE
podré

FUTURE PERFECT
habré podido

CONDITIONAL
podría

CONDITIONAL PERFECT
habría/hubiera podido

PRESENT SUBJUNCTIVE
pueda
puedas
pueda
podamos
podáis
puedan

PERFECT SUBJUNCTIVE
haya podido

IMPERFECT SUBJUNCTIVE
pudiera/pudiese

PLUPERFECT SUBJUNCTIVE
hubiera/hubiese podido

¿*Se puede* telefonear de aquí?

Can one telephone from here?

Los alpinistas *no pudieron* llegar hasta la cima porque nevó.

The mountaineers *were unable* to get to the top because it snowed.

¡No *podría* vivir sin ti!

*I could*n't live without you!

Mañana *podréis* ver el mar por primera vez.

Tomorrow *you will be able to* see the sea for the first time.

Aunque *pueda*, no iré.

Even if *I can*, I won't go.

place; put; switch on

(pg)

GERUND	PAST PARTICIPLE
poniendo	puesto

PRESENT INDICATIVE	PRESENT PERFECT
pongo	he puesto
pones	
pone	
ponemos	
ponéis	
ponen	

PRESENT PROGRESSIVE	IMPERFECT PROGRESSIVE
estoy poniendo	estaba poniendo

IMPERFECT INDICATIVE	PRETERITE
ponía	puse
	pusiste
	puso
	pusimos
	pusisteis
	pusieron

Similar verbs

componer	compose, fix	**oponer(se)**	oppose,
descomponer	break down,		stand out against
	decompose	**posponer**	postpone
disponer	dispose of,	**proponer**	propose
	have available	**reponerse**	get fit, recover
imponer	impose	**suponer**	suppose
indisponer	indispose	**trasponer**	transpose

Note: This highly irregular verb has the following features:

• the first person singular form of the present tense, and therefore all forms of the present subjunctive tense have the stem **pong-;**
• the preterite is **pretérito grave**, with the stem **pus-,** which is also used in the imperfect subjunctive forms;
• the past participle is irregular (**puesto**);
• the singular informal imperative is **pon;**
• the stem for the future and conditional tenses is **pondr-.**

IMPERATIVE
(tú) pon
(usted) ponga

(vosotros) poned
(ustedes) pongan

PLUPERFECT	**PAST ANTERIOR**
había puesto	hube puesto

FUTURE
pondré

FUTURE PERFECT
habré puesto

CONDITIONAL
pondría

CONDITIONAL PERFECT
habría/hubiera puesto

PRESENT SUBJUNCTIVE
ponga
pongas
ponga
pongamos
pongáis
pongan

PERFECT SUBJUNCTIVE
haya puesto

IMPERFECT SUBJUNCTIVE
pusiera/pusiese

PLUPERFECT SUBJUNCTIVE
hubiera/hubiese puesto

Nos mudamos

Querida, *vamos* a *poner* las plantas en tu auto, ¿no? Ya *he puesto* las maletas en el mío. Sí señor, *ponga* la mesa en el camión. Al llegar, *pondremos* todo en el comedor, ¿de acuerdo? ¿Dónde están las llaves de la casa? Creo que las *puse* en el auto. Miguel, *ponte* el abrigo, hace frío.

We move

Darling, *we're going to put* the plants in your car, aren't we? *I've* already *put* the suitcases in mine. Yes, sir, *put* the table in the truck. When we arrive, *we'll put* everything in the dining room, OK? Where are the keys to the house? I think *I put* them in the car. Michael, *put* your coat on, it's cold.

48 querer   want; wish; love

(pg)

GERUND	PAST PARTICIPLE
queriendo	querido

PRESENT INDICATIVE	PRESENT PERFECT
quiero	he querido
quieres	
quiere	
queremos	
queréis	
quieren	

PRESENT PROGRESSIVE	IMPERFECT PROGRESSIVE
estoy queriendo	estaba queriendo

IMPERFECT INDICATIVE	PRETERITE
quería	quise
	quisiste
	quiso
	quisimos
	quisisteis
	quisieron

Note: This verb has the following irregularities:

- it is a stem-changing verb with **-e-** changing to **-ie-** when stressed;
- in addition, it has a **pretérito grave** with the stem **quis-**, also used in the imperfect subjunctive forms;
- the future and conditional stem is **querr-**.

IMPERATIVE
(tú) quiere   (vosotros) quered
(usted) quiera   (ustedes) quieran

PLUPERFECT   **PAST ANTERIOR**
había querido   hube querido

FUTURE   **FUTURE PERFECT**
querré   habré querido

CONDITIONAL   **CONDITIONAL PERFECT**
querría   habría/hubiera querido

PRESENT SUBJUNCTIVE   **PERFECT SUBJUNCTIVE**
quiera   haya querido
quieras
quiera
queramos
queráis
quieran

IMPERFECT SUBJUNCTIVE   **PLUPERFECT SUBJUNCTIVE**
quisiera/quisiese   hubiera/hubiese querido

Te *quiero* más de lo que *tú* me *quieres* a mi.	*I love* you more than *you love* me.
¡*Queremos* pan!	*We want* some bread!
Tienes que hacerlo, *quieras* o no.	You have to do it whether *you want to* or not.
Quisiéramos ir a Granada en primavera.	*We'd want to* go to Granada in the spring.
No sé si mi hermana *querrá* venir a la fiesta.	I don't know if my sister *will want to* come to the party.
Yo *quería* quedarme en casa, pero no pude.	I *wanted to* stay at home, but I couldn't.

GERUND	**PAST PARTICIPLE**
riendo	reído

PRESENT INDICATIVE	**PRESENT PERFECT**
río	he reído
ríes	
ríe	
reímos	
reís	
ríen	

PRESENT PROGRESSIVE	**IMPERFECT PROGRESSIVE**
estoy riendo	estaba riendo

IMPERFECT INDICATIVE	**PRETERITE**
reía	reí
	reiste
	rió
	reímos
	reísteis
	rieron

Similar verb

sonreír　　　smile

Note:　　This verb is actually a type 3 stem-changing verb like **pedir,** but any form with a stressed **-i-** needs an accent.

IMPERATIVE
(tú) ríe   (vosotros) reíd
(usted) ría   (ustedes) rían

PLUPERFECT
había reído

PAST ANTERIOR
hube reído

FUTURE
reiré

FUTURE PERFECT
habré reído

CONDITIONAL
reiría

CONDITIONAL PERFECT
habría/hubiera reído

PRESENT SUBJUNCTIVE
ría
rías
ría
riamos
riais
rían

PERFECT SUBJUNCTIVE
haya reído

IMPERFECT SUBJUNCTIVE
riera/riese

PLUPERFECT SUBJUNCTIVE
hubiera/hubiese reído

¡No *te rías* de mí!   *Do*n't *laugh* at me!

¡No me hagas *reír*!   Don't make me *laugh*!

Ríete niño, no llores más.   *Laugh*, child, don't cry anymore.

La joven te *sonrió* antes de salir.   The young woman *smiled* at you before going out.

Reían como locos.   *They were laughing* like mad.

El público *se está riendo* mucho.   The audience *is laughing* very much.

50 romper(se)   break

GERUND	***PAST PARTICIPLE***
rompiendo	roto

PRESENT INDICATIVE	***PRESENT PERFECT***
rompo	he roto
rompes	
rompe	
rompemos	
rompéis	
rompen	

PRESENT PROGRESSIVE	***IMPERFECT PROGRESSIVE***
estoy rompiendo	estaba rompiendo

IMPERFECT INDICATIVE	***PRETERITE***
rompía	rompí
	rompiste
	rompió
	rompimos
	rompisteis
	rompieron

Note: This verb's only irregularity is its past participle, **roto**.

IMPERATIVE
(tú) rompe   (vosotros) romped
(usted) rompa   (ustedes) rompan

PLUPERFECT   *PAST ANTERIOR*
había roto   hube roto

FUTURE   *FUTURE PERFECT*
romperé   habré roto

CONDITIONAL   *CONDITIONAL PERFECT*
rompería   habría/hubiera roto

PRESENT SUBJUNCTIVE   *PERFECT SUBJUNCTIVE*
rompa   haya roto
rompas
rompa
rompamos
rompáis
rompan

IMPERFECT SUBJUNCTIVE   *PLUPERFECT SUBJUNCTIVE*
rompiera/rompiese   hubiera/hubiese roto

Mi amiga *se rompió* la pierna en el accidente.

My friend *broke* her leg in the accident.

¡No *me rompas* el cuaderno!

Don't break my notebook!

Todas las ventanas *estaban rotas.*

All of the windows *were broken.*

El borracho *está rompiendo* botellas en el bar.

The drunken man *is breaking* bottles in the bar.

51 saber   know; know how to; learn

(pg)

GERUND	PAST PARTICIPLE
sabiendo	sabido

PRESENT INDICATIVE	PRESENT PERFECT
sé	he sabido
sabes	
sabe	
sabemos	
sabéis	
saben	

PRESENT PROGRESSIVE	IMPERFECT PROGRESSIVE
estoy sabiendo	estaba sabiendo

IMPERFECT INDICATIVE	PRETERITE
sabía	supe
	supiste
	supo
	supimos
	supisteis
	supieron

Note: This verb has four irregularities:

- the first person singular form of the present indicative tense, **sé;**
- the whole of the present subjunctive tense, based on the stem **sep-;**
- the **pretérito grave** with the stem **sup-,** also used for the imperfect subjunctive forms;
- the future tense stem **sabr-,** also used in the conditional forms.

Note that in its preterite forms, this verb means *to learn.*

IMPERATIVE

(tú) sabe	(vosotros) sabed
(usted) sepa	(ustedes) sepan

PLUPERFECT
había sabido

PAST ANTERIOR
hube sabido

FUTURE
sabré

FUTURE PERFECT
habré sabido

CONDITIONAL
sabría

CONDITIONAL PERFECT
habría/hubiera sabido

PRESENT SUBJUNCTIVE
sepa
sepas
sepa
sepamos
sepáis
sepan

PERFECT SUBJUNCTIVE
haya sabido

IMPERFECT SUBJUNCTIVE
supiera/supiese

PLUPERFECT SUBJUNCTIVE
hubiera/hubiese sabido

¡No *sabes* nada!	*You do*n't *know* anything!
Que *yo sepa*, el niño tendría unos diez años.	As far as *I know*, the child would be about ten years old.
Sabes **esquiar, ¿verdad?**	*You do know how to* ski, don't you?
Al llegar a casa, *supe* que mi tía había muerto.	When I got home, *I learned* that my aunt had died.
Sí, sí, ya lo *sé*.	Yes, yes, *I know* it.

GERUND saliendo	**PAST PARTICIPLE** salido

PRESENT INDICATIVE salgo sales sale salimos salís salen	**PRESENT PERFECT** he salido

PRESENT PROGRESSIVE estoy saliendo	**IMPERFECT PROGRESSIVE** estaba saliendo

IMPERFECT INDICATIVE salía	**PRETERITE** salí saliste salió salimos salisteis salieron

Note: This verb has three irregularities:

• the first person singular form of the present indicative tense, and so all forms of the present subjunctive tense, which have the stem **salg-**;
• the singular informal imperative is **sal**;
• the irregular stem **saldr-,** used for the future and conditional tenses.

IMPERATIVE	
(tú) sal	(vosotros) salid
(usted) salga	(ustedes) salgan

PLUPERFECT	*PAST ANTERIOR*
había salido	hube salido
FUTURE	*FUTURE PERFECT*
saldré	habré salido
CONDITIONAL	*CONDITIONAL PERFECT*
saldría	habría/hubiera salido
PRESENT SUBJUNCTIVE	*PERFECT SUBJUNCTIVE*
salga	haya salido
salgas	
salga	
salgamos	
salgáis	
salgan	
IMPERFECT SUBJUNCTIVE	*PLUPERFECT SUBJUNCTIVE*
saliera/saliese	hubiera/hubiese salido

¡*Sal* de ahí!	*Get out* of there!
No *salgo* mucho, pues no tengo tiempo, pero *saldremos* mañana si quieres.	*I* don't *go out* much, because I don't have time, but *we'll go out* tomorrow if you want.
***Salgan* con cuidado, por favor.**	*Get out* carefully, please.
Espero que todo *salga* bien.	I hope everything *comes out* well.

GERUND	PAST PARTICIPLE
siendo	sido

PRESENT INDICATIVE	PRESENT PERFECT
soy	he sido
eres	
es	
somos	
sois	
son	

PRESENT PROGRESSIVE	IMPERFECT PROGRESSIVE
estoy siendo	estaba siendo

IMPERFECT INDICATIVE	PRETERITE
era	fui
eras	fuiste
era	fue
éramos	fuimos
erais	fuisteis
eran	fueron

Note: This highly irregular verb should be learned thoroughly, noting the following features:

• the first person singular form of the present indicative tense is **soy,** and the rest of the forms of this tense are highly irregular, as it happens with the imperative forms;
• the present subjunctive tense is based on the form **sea;**
• the preterite tense is highly irregular, and its stem is used for the imperfect subjunctive tense (in both of these, **ser** shares its forms with **ir**);
• the imperfect tense is based on the form **era;**
• other tenses are apparently regular: the gerund, the past participle, the future, and the conditional.

Note also that **ser** is used to form the passive, together with the past participle of the main verb [The Verb System in Spanish].

IMPERATIVE
(tú) sé
(usted) sea

(vosotros) sed
(ustedes) sean

PLUPERFECT
había sido

PAST ANTERIOR
hube sido

FUTURE
seré

FUTURE PERFECT
habré sido

CONDITIONAL
sería

CONDITIONAL PERFECT
habría / hubiera sido

PRESENT SUBJUNCTIVE
sea
seas
sea
seamos
seáis
sean

PERFECT SUBJUNCTIVE
haya sido

IMPERFECT SUBJUNCTIVE
fuera / fuese

PLUPERFECT SUBJUNCTIVE
hubiera / hubiese sido

¡*Sé* bueno, o me enfadaré contigo!

Be good or I'll get angry at you!

Hemos sido amigos desde hace años.

We've been friends for years.

Eran las dos de la tarde.

It was two in the afternoon.

Soy soltero, ¡pero espero que no lo sea para siempre!

I'm a bachelor, but I hope *I won't* always *be* one!

Fueron cinco niños los que ganaron el concurso.

There were five children who won the contest.

Si yo fuera más joven, dormiría menos.

If *I were* younger, I would sleep less.

(pg)

GERUND	PAST PARTICIPLE
teniendo	tenido

PRESENT INDICATIVE	PRESENT PERFECT
tengo	he tenido
tienes	
tiene	
tenemos	
tenéis	
tienen	

PRESENT PROGRESSIVE	IMPERFECT PROGRESSIVE
estoy teniendo	estaba teniendo

IMPERFECT INDICATIVE	PRETERITE
tenía	tuve
	tuviste
	tuvo
	tuvimos
	tuvisteis
	tuvieron

Similar verbs

abstenerse	abstain	**entretener**	entertain
contener	contain, hold	**mantener**	maintain, provide
detener	stop, detain, arrest		for, support
sostener	hold up, support, sustain	**obtener**	get, obtain

Note: The main irregular features of this verb are:

• the first person singular form of the present tense is **tengo**, and so the present subjunctive forms have the stem **teng-**;
• the rest of the present indicative forms behave like an **e** → **ie** stem-changing verb;
• the **pretérito grave** stem is **tuv-**, also used for the imperfect subjunctive forms;
• the future and conditional stem is **tendr-**;
• the singular informal imperative is **ten**.

IMPERATIVE

(tú) ten

(usted) tenga

(vosotros) tened

(ustedes) tengan

PLUPERFECT	PAST ANTERIOR
había tenido	hube tenido

FUTURE	FUTURE PERFECT
tendré	habré tenido

CONDITIONAL	CONDITIONAL PERFECT
tendría	habría/hubiera tenido

PRESENT SUBJUNCTIVE

tenga

tengas

tenga

tengamos

tengáis

tengan

PERFECT SUBJUNCTIVE

haya tenido

IMPERFECT SUBJUNCTIVE	PLUPERFECT SUBJUNCTIVE
tuviera/tuviese	hubiera/hubiese tenido

Tenemos prisa. — *We're in a hurry.*

Tenga piedad de nosotros. — *Have mercy on us.*

Ha tenido mucho que hacer. — *She has had a lot to do.*

Teníamos mucho dinero. — *We had a lot of money.*

Tuvieron que salir. — *They had to go out.*

Si tuviera dinero, lo compraría. — *If I had money, I would buy it.*

Tendremos que trabajar todo el fin de semana. — *We will have to work all weekend.*

55 traer   bring; fetch

(pg)

GERUND	PAST PARTICIPLE
trayendo	traído

PRESENT INDICATIVE	PRESENT PERFECT
traigo	he traído
traes	
trae	
traemos	
traéis	
traen	

PRESENT PROGRESSIVE	IMPERFECT PROGRESSIVE
estoy trayendo	estaba trayendo

INDICATIVE IMPERFECT	PRETERITE
traía	traje
	trajiste
	trajo
	trajimos
	trajisteis
	trajeron

Similar verbs

atraer	attract, lure	**distraer**	distract
contraer	contract	**sustraer**	subtract

Note: The irregular features of this verb are:

• the first person singular form of the present indicative tense is
traigo, making the present subjunctive stem **traig-;**
• the **pretérito grave** stem is **traj-,** used also for the imperfect subjunctive forms; note the missing **-i-** of the third person plural form;
• any form with an ending beginning with **-i-** has a **-y-** instead (except
for the third person plural form of the preterite tense as explained
above);
• the **-i-** of the past participle needs an accent.

156

IMPERATIVE
(tú) trae
(usted) traiga

(vosotros) traed
(ustedes) traigan

PLUPERFECT
había traído

PAST ANTERIOR
hube traído

FUTURE
traeré

FUTURE PERFECT
habré traído

CONDITIONAL
traería

CONDITIONAL PERFECT
habría/hubiera traido

PRESENT SUBJUNCTIVE
traiga
traigas
traiga
traigamos
traigáis
traigan

PERFECT SUBJUNCTIVE
haya traído

IMPERFECT SUBJUNCTIVE
trajera/trajese

PLUPERFECT SUBJUNCTIVE
hubiera/hubiese traído

Tráigame más pan, por favor.

Bring me more bread, please.

Traje sólo veinte pesos.

I only *brought* twenty pesos.

Mi esposa siempre me *traía* un recuerdo de sus viajes.

My wife always *brought* me a souvenir from her trips.

¿*Traerás tú* la comida?

Will you bring the food?

GERUND	PAST PARTICIPLE
valiendo	valido

PRESENT INDICATIVE	PRESENT PERFECT
valgo	he valido
vales	
vale	
valemos	
valéis	
valen	

PRESENT PROGRESSIVE	IMPERFECT PROGRESSIVE
estoy valiendo	estaba valiendo

IMPERFECT INDICATIVE	PRETERITE
valía	valí
	valiste
	valió
	valimos
	valisteis
	valieron

Note: The only irregular features of this verb are:

- the first person singular form of the present indicative tense is **valgo**, making the present subjunctive stem **valg-**;
- the stem of the future and conditional tenses is **valdr-**

IMPERATIVE

(tú) vale   (vosotros) valed
(usted) valga   (ustedes) valgan

PLUPERFECT   *PAST ANTERIOR*
había valido   hube valido

FUTURE   *FUTURE PERFECT*
valdré   habré valido

CONDITIONAL   *CONDITIONAL PERFECT*
valdría   habría / hubiera valido

PRESENT SUBJUNCTIVE   *PERFECT SUBJUNCTIVE*
valga   haya valido
valgas
valga
valgamos
valgáis
valgan

IMPERFECT SUBJUNCTIVE   *PLUPERFECT SUBJUNCTIVE*
valiera / valiese   hubiera / hubiese valido

No *vale* la pena volver.   *It's* not *worth* coming back.

Estas camisas *valían* sólo cinco   These shirts *cost* only five pesos.
pesos.

Si esa pintura *valiera* tanto   If that painting *were worth* as
como sugieres, no la estarían   much as you suggest, they
regalando.   wouldn't be giving it away.

(pg)

GERUND	PAST PARTICIPLE
viniendo	venido

PRESENT INDICATIVE	PRESENT PERFECT
vengo	he venido
vienes	
viene	
venimos	
venís	
vienen	

PRESENT PROGRESSIVE	IMPERFECT PROGRESSIVE
estoy viniendo	estaba viniendo

IMPERFECT INDICATIVE	PRETERITE
venía	vine
	viniste
	vino
	vinimos
	vinisteis
	vinieron

Similar verbs

contravenir	contravene	**intervenir**	intervene
convenir	fit, suit		

Note: The main irregular features of this verb are:

- the first person singular form of the present indicative tense is **vengo,** so the present subjunctive forms have the stem **veng-;**
- the rest of the present indicative forms behave like an **e → ie** stem-changing verb;
- the **pretérito grave** stem is **vin-,** also used for the imperfect subjunctive tense and the gerund,
- the future and conditional stem is **vendr-;**
- the singular informal imperative is **ven.**

IMPERATIVE
(tú) ven
(usted) venga

(vosotros) venid
(ustedes) vengan

PLUPERFECT
había venido

PAST INTERIOR
hube venido

FUTURE
vendré

FUTURE PERFECT
habré venido

CONDITIONAL
vendría

CONDITIONAL PERFECT
habría/hubiera venido

PRESENT SUBJUNCTIVE
venga
vengas
venga
vengamos
vengáis
vengan

PERFECT SUBJUNCTIVE
haya venido

IMPERFECT SUBJUNCTIVE
viniera/viniese

PLUPERFECT SUBJUNCTIVE
hubiera/hubiese venido

Venga conmigo a la comisaría.

Come with me to the police station.

Vinieron en el tren de las doce.

They came on the twelve o'clock train.

Venía a tiempo todos los días.

He came on time every day.

Vendremos a verte mañana.

We'll come to see you tomorrow.

GERUND	PAST PARTICIPLE
viendo	visto

PRESENT INDICATIVE	PRESENT PERFECT
veo	he visto
ves	
ve	
vemos	
veis	
ven	

PRESENT PROGRESSIVE	IMPERFECT PROGRESSIVE
estoy viendo	estaba viendo

IMPERFECT INDICATIVE	PRETERITE
veía	vi
	viste
	vio
	vimos
	visteis
	vieron

Similar verbs

entrever   glimpse   **prever**   foresee, forecast

Note: The main irregular features of this verb are:

• the stem of the first person singular form of the present indicative tense, all of the present subjunctive forms, and the imperfect indicative tense is **ve-**;
• the preterite forms are the same as for **-er** and **-ir** verbs, but with no written accents;
• the past participle is irregular: **visto.**

In other respects, **ver** is regular, but note that the singular informal imperative—**ve**—is identical to that of **ir**.

IMPERATIVE	
(tú) ve	(vosotros) ved
(usted) vea	(ustedes) vean

PLUPERFECT	*PAST ANTERIOR*
había visto	hube visto

FUTURE	*FUTURE PERFECT*
veré	habré visto

CONDITIONAL	*CONDITIONAL PERFECT*
vería	habría/hubiera visto

PRESENT SUBJUNCTIVE	*PERFECT SUBJUNCTIVE*
vea	haya visto
veas	
vea	
veamos	
veáis	
vean	

IMPERFECT SUBJUNCTIVE	*PLUPERFECT SUBJUNCTIVE*
viera/viese	hubiera/hubiese visto

¡Te *veo* claramente!	*I see* you clearly!
Nos *vieron* entrar en el café.	*They saw* us going into the café.
Había *visto* a su madre llorando.	*He had seen* his mother crying.
Estamos *viendo* una película muy buena en la televisión.	*We are watching* a very good movie on television.
Los economistas *prevén* que la inflación aumentará.	The economists *foresee* that inflation will go up.

C
SUBJECT INDEX

SUBJECT INDEX

The numbers given below refer to the relevant section in The Verb System in Spanish.

D
VERB INDEX

An asterisk next to a verb indicates that it is one of the Model Verbs listed in section B.

Whenever the letters **ch**, **ll**, and **ñ** appear, English alphabetical order has been used throughout.

A

abandonar *(tr)*	abandon, desert, leave behind **2**
abastecer *(tr)*	provide, supply **32**
ablandar *(tr)*	soften **2**
abolir *(tr)*	abolish **4**
abordar *(tr)*	approach, board **2**
aborrecer *(tr)*	hate, abhor **32**
abortar *(intr)*	abort, miscarry **2**
abotonar *(tr)*	button **2**
abrasar *(tr)*	scorch **2**
abrazar(se) *(tr/refl)*	embrace, hug **6**
abrevar *(tr)*	water (*animals*) **2**
abreviar(se) *(tr/refl)*	shorten, become shorter **14**
abrigar(se) *(tr/refl)*	shelter **7**
***abrir** *(tr/intr)*	open; open up **25**
abrir *(tr)*	turn on (*faucet/tap*)
abrir con llave *(tr)*	unlock
abrir por la fuerza *(tr)*	force one's way into
abrochar *(tr)*	button, fasten **2**
absolver *(tr)*	absolve, let off **20**
absorber *(tr)*	absorb **3**
abstenerse de *(refl)*	abstain from, refrain from **54**
abultar *(tr)*	increase, enlarge **2**
abundar *(intr)*	abound, be abundant **2**
aburrir *(tr)*	bore **4**
abusar de *(tr)*	misuse, abuse **2**
acabar *(tr)*	finish, complete **2**
acabar con *(tr)*	finish with; do away with
acabar de	have just
acabar(se) *(intr/refl)*	end, finish; end up **2**
acallar *(tr)*	silence **2**
acampar(se) *(intr/refl)*	camp **2**
acanalar *(tr)*	channel **2**
acariciar *(tr)*	caress, pet, fondle, cherish **2**

acarrear *(tr)*	haul **2**
acechar *(tr)*	lie in wait for **2**
acelerar *(tr)*	accelerate, speed up **2**
aceptar *(tr)*	accept **2**
acerar *(tr)*	steel **2**
acercar *(tr)*	bring near **5**
acercarse a *(refl)*	approach **5**
acertar *(tr/intr)*	hit the mark **19**
aclarar *(tr)*	clarify, clear up; rinse **2**
acoger *(tr)*	welcome **11**
acometer *(tr)*	attack; undertake **3**
acomodar *(tr)*	accommodate, lodge, put up; suit **2**
acompañar *(tr)*	accompany **2**
aconsejar *(tr)*	advise **2**
acontecer *(intr)*	happen, occur **32**
acoplar(se) *(tr/refl)*	mate **2**
acordar *(tr)*	tune **20**
acordarse de *(refl)*	remember **20**
acortar(se) *(tr/refl)*	draw in, shorten, become shorter **2**
acosar *(tr)*	harass, hound, pester **2**
acostar *(tr)*	put to bed **20**
acostarse *(refl)*	go to bed, lie (down) **20**
acostumbrar *(tr)*	accustom **2**
acostumbrarse a *(refl)*	become accustomed, get used to **2**
acribillar *(tr)*	riddle; pester **2**
actualizar *(tr)*	modernize, update **6**
***actuar** *(tr/intr)*	act, do, perform **15**
actuar de mimo *(intr)*	mime
acudir *(intr)*	gather around; show up, turn up **4**
acumular(se) *(tr/refl)*	accumulate, collect, mount up **2**
acunar *(tr)*	rock (to sleep) **2**
acuñar *(tr)*	strike (*coin, medal*); wedge **2**
acusar *(tr)*	accuse, charge **2**
adaptar *(tr)*	adapt; suit **2**
adaptarse a *(refl)*	adapt, adjust to **2**

VERB INDEX

agravar(se) *(tr/refl)*	worsen **2**
agraviar *(tr)*	wrong **2**
agregar *(tr)*	add **7**
agriar(se) *(tr/refl)*	sour **14**
aguantar *(tr/intr)*	bear, endure, hold out, put up with **2**
aguar *(tr)*	water/thin down (*wine*, etc.) **8**
aguardar *(tr)*	wait **2**
agujerear *(tr)*	pierce, make a hole in **2**
ahogar(se) *(tr/refl)*	drown; suffocate **7**
ahorrar *(tr)*	put away, save (*money, time*) **2**
ahuecar *(tr)*	hollow out **5**
ahusarse *(refl)*	taper **2**
aislar *(tr)*	isolate **15**
ajustar *(tr)*	adjust, regulate; settle (*accounts*); suit **2**
alabar *(tr)*	praise **2**
alargar(se) *(tr/refl)*	extend, lengthen, stretch **7**
alarmar *(tr)*	alarm, frighten **2**
alborear *(intr)*	dawn **2**
alborotar *(intr)*	make a racket, brawl **2**
alcanzar *(tr/intr)*	reach, get to, attain **6**
alejar *(tr)*	alienate, distance, move away **2**
alejarse *(refl)*	go away **2**
alentar *(tr)*	encourage; breathe **2**
aligerar *(tr)*	lighten **2**
alimentar *(tr)*	feed **2**
alinear(se) *(tr/refl)*	align, line up **2**
alisar *(tr)*	flatten, smooth **2**
alistarse *(refl)*	get ready; join up (*armed services*) **2**
aliviar *(tr)*	alleviate, deaden (*pain*), relieve **2**
allanar *(tr)*	flatten, level, smooth **2**
almacenar *(tr)*	hoard, store **2**
almorzar *(intr)*	have lunch **6, 20**
alojar *(tr)*	accommodate, house, lodge, put up **2**

VERB INDEX

alquilar *(tr)*	charter, let, rent, rent out	**2**
alterar *(tr)*	upset, disturb	**2**
alternar *(intr)*	alternate	**2**
aludir a *(intr)*	refer to	**4**
alumbrar *(tr)*	light (up)	**2**
alzar *(tr)*	hoist, lift, raise	**6**
amalgamar *(tr)*	amalgamate	**2**
amamantar *(tr)*	suckle	**2**
amanecer *(intr)*	dawn	**32**
amansar *(tr)*	tame	**2**
***amar** *(tr)*	love	**1**
amargar *(tr)*	sour	**7**
amarrar *(tr)*	fasten, moor, tie up	**2**
amarrar con una cuerda *(tr)*	rope together	
amenazar *(tr)*	threaten	**6**
amoldar *(tr)*	mold	**2**
amontonar *(tr)*	heap, hoard	**2**
amontonar(se) *(tr/refl)*	huddle, pile	**2**
amortiguar *(tr)*	deaden, muffle	**8**
amortizar *(tr)*	pay off	**6**
amotinarse *(refl)*	riot	**2**
ampliar *(tr)*	enlarge, expand, widen	**14**
amplificar *(tr)*	amplify	**5**
ampollar(se) *(tr/refl)*	blister	**2**
amputar *(tr)*	amputate	**2**
analizar *(tr)*	analyze	**6**
anclar *(intr)*	anchor	**2**
***andar** *(intr)*	walk, go around; function, work	**27**
andar a gatas *(intr)*	crawl, creep	
andar a pasos largos *(intr)*	stride	
andar con paso		
majestuoso *(intr)*	sweep (*movement*)	
aneblarse *(refl)*	become misty	**2**
anestesiar *(tr)*	anesthetize	**2**
anexar *(tr)*	annex	**2**
anhelar *(tr)*	long for	**2**
anidar *(tr/intr)*	nest	**2**
animar *(tr)*	animate, encourage	**2**

animarse *(refl)*	brighten up, cheer up; bear up **2**
aniquilar *(tr)*	annihilate **2**
anochecer *(intr)*	get dark **32**
anotar *(tr)*	write down **2**
anticipar *(tr)*	anticipate; advance (*payment*) **2**
anudar *(tr)*	knot **2**
anular *(tr)*	annul, cancel out, write off (*insurance, debt*) **2**
anunciar *(tr)*	advertise, announce **2**
añadir *(tr)*	add **4**
apacentar *(tr)*	graze **2**
apaciguar *(tr)*	appease, pacify **8**
apagar *(tr)*	extinguish, put out; quench; switch off, turn off **7**
apagarse *(refl)*	go out, die away **7**
aparcar *(tr)*	park **5**
aparecer *(intr)*	appear **32**
aparecer inesperadamente *(intr)*	pop up
aparentar *(tr)*	pretend **2**
apartar *(tr)*	move away; separate **2**
apartarse de *(refl)*	diverge from **2**
apedrear *(tr)*	stone **2**
apelar *(tr/intr)*	appeal **2**
apercibir *(tr)*	catch sight of **4**
apetecer *(tr)*	feel like, want **32**
apilar(se) *(tr/refl)*	pile **3**
aplastar *(tr)*	crush **2**
aplaudir *(tr/intr)*	applaud, clap **4**
aplazar *(tr)*	adjourn, defer, postpone, procrastinate **6**
aplicar *(tr)*	apply **5**
aporrear *(tr)*	bash, beat up **2**
apostar *(tr/intr)*	bet, stake **20**
apoyar *(tr)*	hold up, side with, support, back, back (up); prop, shore up; stand by, uphold **2**

arrodillarse *(refl)*	kneel (down) **2**
arrojar *(tr)*	cast, fling, hurl, pitch, throw **2**
arrollar *(tr/intr)*	coil, roll up **2**
arrugar(se) *(tr/refl)*	wrinkle, ruffle **7**
arruinar *(tr)*	bankrupt, make a mess of, ruin, wreck **2**
asaltar *(tr)*	assault, storm **2**
asar *(tr)*	roast **2**
asar a la parrilla *(tr)*	grill
ascender *(tr)*	advance (*rank*), promote **19**
ascender *(intr)*	ascend, go up **19**
ascender a *(intr)*	add up to, amount to, number
asediar *(tr)*	besiege **2**
asegurar *(tr)*	assure, ensure, make safe, secure, underwrite **2**
asegurar(se) *(tr/refl)*	insure **2**
asentir *(intr)*	agree, assent **19**
asesinar *(tr)*	assassinate, murder, slaughter **2**
asfixiar(se) *(tr/refl)*	suffocate, throttle **2**
asignar *(tr)*	allocate, assign **2**
asimilar *(tr)*	assimilate **2**
***asir(se)** *(tr)*	seize; grasp; grab; snatch **18**
asistir *(tr)*	assist **4**
asistir a *(tr/intr)*	witness; be present at **4**
asociarse *(refl)*	associate, band together **2**
asociarse con *(refl)*	team up with
asolar *(tr)*	devastate **2**
asomar(se) *(tr/refl)*	lean out, stick out **2**
asombrar *(tr)*	amaze, surprise **2**
asombrarse *(refl)*	wonder **2**
aspirar *(intr)*	inhale **2**
aspirar a *(intr)*	aim, aspire **2**
astillar *(tr)*	chip, splinter **2**
asumir *(tr)*	assume **4**
asustar *(tr)*	frighten, scare **2**
asustarse *(refl)*	get scared **2**
atacar *(tr)*	attack **5**
atajar *(tr/intr)*	cut across, intercept **2**

VERB INDEX

atar *(tr)*	tie, tie up **2**
atar con una cuerda *(tr)*	rope together
atender *(tr)*	assist; care for, nurse, tend, treat (*medically*) **19**
atenerse a *(refl)*	abide by, hold to **54**
aterrar *(tr)*	terrify **2**
aterrizar *(intr)*	land **6**
aterrorizar *(tr)*	terrify, terrorize **6**
atiborrarse de comida *(refl)*	stuff oneself with food **2**
atiesar(se) *(tr/refl)*	harden, stiffen, tighten **2**
atomizar *(tr)*	atomize **6**
atormentar *(tr)*	torment **2**
atornillar *(tr)*	screw **2**
atracar *(tr/intr)*	moor, tie up (*nautical*) **5**
atraer *(tr)*	attract, lure **55**
atragantarse *(refl)*	choke **2**
atrancar *(tr)*	bar, bolt (*door*) **5**
atrapar *(tr)*	trap **2**
atravesar *(tr/intr)*	cross, go across; shoot (*rapids*) **19**
atreverse *(refl)*	dare **3**
atropellar *(tr)*	knock over, run down, run over **2**
auditar *(tr)*	audit **2**
aullar *(intr)*	howl **2**
aumentar *(tr/ntr)*	add to, increase, raise, rise **2**
ausentarse *(refl)*	absent oneself, play truant **2**
automatizar *(tr)*	automate **2**
autorizar *(tr)*	authorize, entitle **2**
avanzar *(tr/intr)*	advance, move forward **6**
aventajar *(tr)*	surpass, top **2**
aventurar *(tr)*	gamble, venture **2**
avergonzar(se) *(tr/refl)*	shame; be ashamed **6**
averiarse *(refl)*	get damaged; break down **14**
*averiguar *(tr)*	verify; find out; look up; know **8**
avisar *(tr)*	inform, warn **2**
avistar *(tr)*	sight **2**
ayudar *(tr)*	aid, help **2**
ayunar *(intr)*	fast **2**

azorar *(tr)*	disturb, embarrass, upset	**2**
azotar *(tr)*	whip	**2**
azucarar *(tr)*	sugar, sweeten	**2**

B

babear *(intr)*	dribble	**2**
bailar *(intr)*	dance	**2**
bajar *(tr)*	let down, lower, pull down, take down	**2**
bajar *(intr)*	come down, go down, get down, descend; decline, lessen; ebb *(tide)*, subside *(water)*	**2**
bajar de *(intr)*	alight, get off, get out of	
balancear(se) *(tr/refl)*	rock, sway, swing	**2**
balar *(intr)*	bleat	**2**
balbucear *(tr/intr)*	stammer, stutter	**2**
bambolearse *(intr)*	sway, totter	**2**
banquetear *(tr/intr)*	feast	**2**
bañar *(tr)*	bath, bathe, dip	**2**
bañarse *(refl)*	take a bath	**2**
barrear *(tr)*	barricade	**2**
barrer *(tr)*	sweep	**3**
basar en *(tr)*	base on	**2**
bastar *(intr)*	be enough, do, suffice	**2**
batir *(tr)*	beat; hammer	**4**
bautizar *(tr)*	baptize	**6**
beber *(tr)*	drink	**3**
*bendecir *(tr)*	bless	**28**
beneficiar *(tr)*	benefit, do good to	**2**
besar *(tr)*	kiss	**2**
bifurcarse *(intr)*	fork	**5**
biodegradar(se) *(tr/refl)*	biodegrade	**2**
bizquear *(intr)*	squint	**2**
blandir *(tr)*	brandish, flourish	**4**
blanquear(se) *(tr/refl)*	bleach, whiten	**2**
blasfemar *(intr)*	blaspheme, curse	**2**
bloquear *(tr)*	block, stop, trap	**2**
boicotear *(tr)*	boycott	**2**
bombardear *(tr)*	bomb, bombard, shell	**2**
bombear *(tr)*	pump	**2**

bombearse *(refl)*	bulge, warp	**2**
borbotar *(intr)*	boil over, bubble	**2**
bordar *(tr)*	embroider	**2**
borrar *(tr)*	delete, erase, rub out, scrub, wipe out	**2**
bostezar *(intr)*	yawn	**6**
boxear *(intr)*	box	**2**
bramar *(intr)*	bellow, roar	**2**
brasear *(tr)*	braise	**2**
brillar *(tr/intr)*	gleam, glow, shine	**2**
brincar *(intr)*	hop, skip	**5**
brindar *(tr)*	toast (*with drink*)	**2**
bromear *(intr)*	joke	**2**
broncear(se) *(tr/refl)*	tan	**2**
brotar *(intr)*	spring (from), sprout (from), well up	**2**
burbujear *(intr)*	bubble	**2**
burlar *(tr)*	circumvent, deceive	**2**
buscar *(tr)*	look for, look up, search, seek	**5**

C **cabalgar** *(tr/intr)*	ride (*horse*)	**7**
cabecear *(intr)*	nod (*sleepily*), shake one's head	**2**
***caber** *(intr)*	fit	**29**
caducar *(tr)*	fall due; expire	**5**
***caer(se)** *(intr)*	fall, drop	**30**
caer enfermo *(intr)*	fall ill	
calar *(tr)*	go through, penetrate	**2**
calar(se) *(tr/refl)*	drench, soak	**2**
calcular *(tr)*	calculate, compute	**2**
calentar(se) *(tr/refl)*	heat, warm, warm up	**19**
calificar *(tr)*	define, call, describe, qualify	**5**
callarse *(refl)*	shut up	
calmar(se) *(tr/refl)*	calm (down), cool (down)	**2**
calumniar *(tr)*	slander	**2**
calzar *(tr)*	put shoes on, shoe	**6**
cambiar *(tr/intr)*	change, exchange, switch, vary; shift (e.g., *weather*)	**2**

cambiar por *(tr)*	trade, exchange
cambiarse *(refl)*	change into, turn **2**
caminar *(intr)*	step, walk **2**
cancelar *(tr)*	call off, cancel, write off (*insurance, debt*) **2**
cansar(se) *(tr/refl)*	tire **2**
cantar *(tr/intr)*	sing **2**
canturrear *(intr)*	hum (*person*) **2**
capturar *(tr)*	capture **2**
caracterizar *(tr)*	characterize **6**
carecer *(intr)*	lack **32**
cargar *(tr)*	charge, load; debit (*account*) **7**
caricaturizar *(tr)*	caricature **6**
casar(se) *(tr/refl)*	get married, marry **2**
castigar *(tr)*	punish **7**
catalogar *(tr)*	catalogue, list **7**
causar *(tr)*	cause **2**
cavar *(tr/intr)*	dig **2**
*****cazar** *(tr/intr)*	hunt, chase **6**
cazar ilegalmente *(tr)*	poach
cebar *(tr)*	fatten, feed **2**
cebar *(intr)*	grip, catch (*nut*) **2**
ceder *(tr/intr)*	cede, compromise, give in, give up, yield **3**
ceder el paso *(intr)*	give way
cegar *(tr)*	blind **7, 19**
celebrar *(tr)*	celebrate **2**
cenar *(tr/intr)*	dine, have supper **2**
censurar *(tr)*	censor, censure **2**
centellear *(intr)*	sparkle **2**
centralizar *(tr)*	centralize **6**
centrifugar *(tr)*	spin **7**
ceñir *(tr)*	skirt, surround **17**
cepillar *(tr)*	brush **2**
cercar *(tr)*	circle, close in, enclose, fence (in), surround **5**
cercar con un seto *(tr)*	hedge
cerrar(se) *(tr/refl)*	close, shut; turn off (*faucet*) **19**
cerrar con llave *(tr)*	lock

colgar *(tr/intr)*	hang, hang up **7, 20**
colmar *(tr)*	fill up **2**
colocar *(tr)*	place **5**
colorear *(tr)*	color **2**
combatir *(tr)*	combat, fight **4**
combinar(se) *(tr/refl)*	combine **2**
comentar *(tr/intr)*	comment, remark **2**
comenzar *(tr/intr)*	begin, start, get started **6, 19**
*comer *(tr/intr)*	eat, have (*to eat*) **3**
comercializar *(tr)*	commercialize, market **6**
comerciar *(tr/intr)*	deal, trade **2**
cometer *(tr)*	commit **3**
comisionar *(tr)*	commission **2**
compadecer(se) de *(tr/refl)*	pity, sympathize, take pity on **32**
comparar *(tr)*	compare **2**
compartir *(tr)*	share **4**
compensar *(tr)*	compensate **2**
competir *(intr)*	compete; race **24**
compilar *(tr)*	compile **2**
completar *(tr)*	complete **2**
complicar *(tr)*	complicate **5**
componer *(tr)*	compose; fix **47**
componerse de *(refl)*	be composed of, consist (*of*) 47
comportarse *(refl)*	behave **2**
*comprar *(tr)*	buy, purchase; take over (*business*) **2**
comprender *(tr)*	comprise; understand **2**
comprimir *(tr)*	compress **4**
comprobar *(tr)*	check, verify **20**
comprometerse a *(refl)*	commit oneself to **3**
computar *(tr)*	compute **2**
comulgar *(tr/intr)*	administer/take communion **7**
comunicar *(tr/intr)*	communicate **5**
concebir *(tr)*	conceive **4**
conceder *(tr)*	allow, award (*prize*), concede, cede; confer, grant **3**
concentrarse *(refl)*	concentrate, gather; center on **2**

VERB INDEX

concernir *(tr)*	concern	**19**
concluir *(tr/intr)*	conclude, close *(sale)*, finish	**12**
concordar con *(intr)*	accord with	**20**
condenar *(tr)*	condemn, convict, damn	**2**
condensar *(tr)*	condense	**2**
condimentar *(tr)*	condiment, flavor, season	**2**
condolerse *(refl)*	sympathize	**20**
***conducir** *(tr)*	drive; lead; conduct	**31**
conducirse *(refl)*	behave	**31**
conectar *(tr)*	connect, switch on	**2**
confeccionar *(tr)*	make out *(list)*; tailor	**2**
conferenciar *(intr)*	be in conference, confer	**12**
confesar *(tr)*	confess	**19**
confiar *(tr/intr)*	confide, entrust, trust	**14**
confinar *(tr)*	confine, border on	**2**
confirmar *(tr)*	confirm	**2**
confiscar *(tr)*	confiscate	**5**
conformarse a *(refl)*	conform to; comply with	**2**
conformarse con *(refl)*	resign onself to	**2**
confortar *(tr)*	comfort	**2**
confrontar *(tr)*	confront	**2**
confundir *(tr)*	confuse, muddle up, puzzle	**4**
congregar(se) *(tr/refl)*	congregate, gather	**7**
conjurar *(intr)*	conjure	**2**
conmemorar *(tr)*	commemorate	**2**
conocer *(tr)*	know *(person, place)*; get to know; meet	**32**
conquistar *(tr)*	conquer	**2**
conseguir *(tr/intr)*	achieve; attain, come by	**10, 24**
conservar *(tr)*	conserve, preserve, retain	**2**
considerar *(tr)*	consider, look on, regard, think over	**2**
consistir en *(intr)*	consist of	**4**
consolar *(tr)*	console	**20**
consolidar *(tr)*	consolidate	**2**
conspirar *(intr)*	conspire, plot	**2**
constar de *(intr)*	consist of, comprise	**2**
consternar *(tr)*	dismay	**2**
constituir *(tr)*	constitute	**12**

construir *(tr)*	build, construct, erect, make **12**
consultar *(tr)*	consult, go and see (e.g., *doctor*) **2**
consumir *(tr)*	consume **4**
contactar *(tr)*	contact **2**
contagiar(se) *(tr/refl)*	become infected, infect **2**
contaminar *(tr)*	contaminate, pollute **2**
contar *(tr)*	count, number; check off; relate, tell **20**
contar con *(intr)*	count on, depend on
contemplar *(tr/intr)*	contemplate, gaze at view **2**
contener(se) *(tr/refl)*	contain, hold; hold back **54**
contentar *(tr)*	please **2**
contestar *(tr)*	answer, rejoin, reply **2**
continuar *(tr/intr)*	carry on, continue **15**
contradecir(se) *(tr/refl)*	contradict (oneself) **34**
contraer(se) *(tr/refl)*	contract; shrink **55**
contrahacer *(tr)*	copy, imitate **41**
contrastar *(tr)*	contrast **2**
contratar *(tr)*	hire **2**
contravenir *(tr)*	contravene **57**
contribuir *(tr)*	contribute **12**
controlar *(tr)*	control, inspect, monitor **2**
contundir *(tr)*	bruise **4**
convencer *(tr)*	convince, bring around **9**
convenir *(tr)*	fit, suit; agree **57**
conversar *(intr)*	converse **2**
convertir *(tr)*	convert, transform **22**
convertirse en *(refl)*	turn into **22**
convidar *(tr)*	invite, treat **2**
convivir *(intr)*	coexist **4**
convocar *(tr)*	call a meeting, summon **5**
cooperar *(intr)*	cooperate **2**
coordinar *(tr)*	coordinate **2**
copiar *(tr)*	copy **2**
coquetear *(intr)*	flirt **2**
coronar *(tr)*	cap, crown **2**
corregir *(tr)*	correct **11, 24**
correr *(intr)*	run, flow, race, slip, stream **3**

corresponder *(intr)*	correspond **3**
corroer(se) *(tr/refl)*	corrode, erode, rust **30**
corromper(se) *(tr/refl)*	corrupt, decay, rot **3**
cortar *(tr/intr)*	cut, chop, mow, slice, trim; turn off, switch off; turn out; break in (*conversation*) **2**
cortejar *(tr)*	court, woo **2**
cosechar *(tr)*	harvest, reap **2**
coser *(tr)*	sew, stitch **3**
cosquillear *(tr)*	tickle **2**
costar *(intr)*	cost **20**
cotizar *(tr)*	quote, price, value **6**
crear *(tr)*	create **2**
crecer *(intr)*	grow **32**
creer *(tr)*	believe **13**
crepitar *(intr)*	crackle, sizzle **2**
criar *(tr)*	bring up (*children*) **14**
cristalizar *(tr)*	crystallize **6**
criticar *(tr)*	criticize **5**
croar *(intr)*	croak **2**
cronometrar *(tr)*	time **2**
crucificar *(tr)*	crucify **5**
crujir *(intr)*	crack, creak, crunch, rustle **4**
cruzar *(tr)*	bridge, cross **6**
cuadrar *(tr)*	square **2**
cuantificar *(tr)*	quantity **5**
cubicar *(tr)*	cube **5**
cubrir *(tr)*	cover **25**
cuchichear *(intr)*	whisper **2**
cuestionar *(tr)*	interrogate, question **2**
cuidar *(tr)*	look after, nurse, take care of **2**
culpar *(tr)*	blame **2**
cultivar *(tr/intr)*	cultivate, farm, grow **2**
cumplir *(tr)*	carry out, fulfill, perform, keep to (*promise*) **4**
curar *(tr)*	cure, heal **2**

D

***dar** *(tr)*	give **33**
dar los naipes *(tr)*	deal cards

dar a luz *(tr)*	give birth
dar cuerda *(tr)*	wind
dar de comer *(tr)*	feed
dar entrada *(tr)*	admit, allow in
dar fruto *(intr)*	bear fruit
dar guerra *(tr)*	bother, play up
dar gusto *(tr)*	please
dar la bienvenida *(tr)*	welcome
dar la hora *(intr)*	strike *(hour)*
dar las gracias *(tr)*	thank
dar marcha atrás *(intr)*	back, reverse *(car)*
dar razón *(tr)*	account for
dar resultado *(intr)*	give results
dar testimonio de *(tr)*	bear witness to
dar un paso *(intr)*	step
dar un puntapié *(tr)*	kick
dar un salto mortal *(intr)*	somersault
dar una palmada *(tr)*	slap
dar voces *(intr)*	call out, shout out
dar vueltas *(intr)*	circle
darse cuenta de *(refl)*	realize
darse prisa *(refl)*	hurry, make haste
datar de *(intr)*	date from **2**
deambular *(intr)*	saunter; wander **2**
debatir *(tr)*	debate **4**
deber *(tr)*	owe **3**
deber *(intr)*	have to, must, ought, should **3**
debilitar(se) *(tr/refl)*	weaken; wilt **2**
decaer *(intr)*	decay, decline **30**
decepcionar *(tr)*	disappoint **2**
decidir *(tr)*	decide **4**
decidirse *(refl)*	make up one's mind **4**
*decir *(tr/intr)*	say; tell **34**
declarar *(tr/intr)*	declare, state **2**
decorar *(tr)*	decorate **2**
decretar *(tr)*	decree **2**
dedicar *(tr)*	dedicate **5**
dedicarse a *(tr/refl)*	dedicate oneself to, devote oneself to **5**

VERB INDEX

desafiar *(tr)*	challenge **14**
desagregarse *(refl)*	disintegrate **7**
desaguar *(tr)*	drain **8**
desalentar *(tr)*	discourage **2**
desamarrar *(tr)*	cast off, untie (*boat*) **2**
desamparar *(tr)*	abandon **2**
desanimar *(tr)*	discourage **2**
desaparecer *(intr)*	disappear, vanish **32**
desaprobar *(intr)*	disapprove **20**
desarmar *(tr)*	disarm **2**
desarrollar(se) *(tr/refl)*	develop, evolve **2**
desatar *(tr)*	undo, untie **2**
desatascar *(tr)*	unblock (*commerce*) **5**
desatender *(tr)*	neglect **19**
desayunar *(tr/intr)*	have breakfast **2**
desbloquear *(tr)*	unblock (*commerce*) **2**
desbordar(se) *(intr/refl)*	flood, overflow **2**
descalzar(se) *(tr/refl)*	take off (*shoes*) **6**
descansar *(tr/intr)*	repose, rest **2**
descargar *(tr/intr)*	discharge, download (*computing*), dump, unload **7**
descascarar *(tr)*	shell (*eggs*) **2**
descender *(intr)*	come down, descend, go down **19**
descifrar *(tr)*	decipher, decode **2**
descolgar *(tr)*	lift (*receiver*), unhook; take down **7, 20**
descolorar *(intr)*	fade **2**
descomponer(se) *(tr/refl)*	decompose; break down **47**
desconcertar *(tr)*	embarrass, throw off balance **19**
desconectar *(tr)*	disconnect, switch off, turn off **2**
desconfiar de *(tr)*	distrust **14**
descongelar *(tr)*	defrost, thaw, deice **2**
desconocer *(tr)*	be ignorant; deny **32**
descontar *(tr)*	deduct, discount **20**
describir *(tr)*	describe **37**
descubrir *(tr)*	discover, find out, strike (*oil*), uncover **25**

desmigajar(se) *(tr/refl)*	crumble **2**
desmontar *(tr)*	dismantle (e.g., *tent*), take down **2**
desmoronarse *(refl)*	fall apart **2**
desnudar(se) *(tr/refl)*	bare, strip off, undress **2**
desobedecer *(tr/intr)*	disobey **32**
desobstruir *(tr)*	unblock **12**
desoír *(tr)*	ignore, turn a deaf ear to **44**
desollar *(tr)*	skin **20**
desorganizar *(tr)*	disorganize **6**
despachar *(tr)*	dispatch, send off **2**
desparramarse *(refl)*	scatter **2**
despedir *(tr)*	dismiss, fire **24**
despedir(se) *(tr/refl)*	say good-bye to, take leave of **24**
despegar *(tr/intr)*	lift off (*rocket*), take off; take down (e.g., *poster*); detach, unstick **7**
despejar(se) *(tr/refl)*	brighten up, clear **2**
despellejar *(tr)*	skin **2**
despertar(se) *(tr/refl)*	awaken, wake up **19**
despilfarrar *(tr)*	waste **2**
desplazar *(tr)*	displace **6**
desplazar hacia arriba *(tr)*	scroll up
desplazar hacia abajo *(tr)*	scroll down
desplegar *(tr)*	display **7, 19**
despojar(se) de *(tr/refl)*	take away from; shed, take off **2**
despreciar *(tr)*	scorn **2**
destacar(se) *(tr/refl)*	be noticeable, highlight; stand out **5**
destapar *(tr)*	uncover **2**
destellar *(intr)*	flash, sparkle **2**
desterrar *(tr)*	banish, exile **19**
destilar *(tr)*	distill **2**
destornillar *(tr)*	unscrew **2**
destruir *(tr)*	destroy **12**
desvalorizar *(tr)*	devalue **6**
desviar *(intr)*	divert **14**
desviar(se) de *(refl)*	detour, deviate, skew **14**

detallar *(tr)*	detail **2**
detectar *(tr)*	detect **2**
detener(se) *(tr/refl)*	stop; arrest, detain **54**
deteriorar *(intr)*	deteriorate **2**
determinar *(tr)*	determine **2**
detestar *(tr)*	detest, hate **2**
devaluar *(tr)*	devalue **15**
devastar *(tr)*	devastate **2**
devolver *(tr)*	give back, hand back, pay back; return, send back, take back (*goods*) **20**
devolverse *(refl)*	go back **20**
devorar *(tr)*	devour **2**
diagnosticar *(tr)*	diagnose **5**
dibujar *(tr)*	draw **2**
dictar *(tr)*	dictate **2**
difamar *(tr)*	slander **2**
diferenciar *(tr)*	differentiate **2**
diferenciarse *(refl)*	be different **2**
diferir *(intr)*	differ **22**
dificultar *(tr)*	hinder **2**
difundir *(tr)*	diffuse, spread **4**
digerir *(tr)*	digest **22**
dignarse *(refl)*	deign to **2**
diluir *(tr)*	dilute **12**
dimitir *(tr)*	resign **4**
diputar *(tr)*	delegate, deputize **2**
dirigir *(tr)*	address (e.g., *letter*); direct, manage, steer **11**
dirigirse a/hacia *(refl)*	address (*a person*)/make for, head for **11**
discernir *(tr)*	discern **19**
disciplinar *(tr)*	discipline **2**
disculpar *(tr)*	excuse, exonerate; forgive **2**
disculparse *(refl)*	apologize **2**
discutir *(tr/intr)*	argue, debate, discuss **4**
diseminar *(tr)*	disseminate, spread **2**
diseñar *(tr)*	design, style **2**
disfrazar *(tr)*	disguise **6**

disfrutar *(tr)*	enjoy **2**
disgregarse *(refl)*	disintegrate **7**
disimular *(tr)*	conceal; pretend **2**
dislocarse *(refl)*	dislocate **5**
disminuir *(tr/intr)*	diminish, decrease, lessen **12**
disolver(se) *(tr/refl)*	dissolve **20**
disparar *(tr/intr)*	fire, shoot **2**
dispensar *(tr)*	exempt, pardon **2**
dispersar(se) *(tr/refl)*	disperse, scatter **2**
disponer de *(tr)*	dispose of; have available **47**
disputar *(tr/intr)*	argue, dispute **2**
*distinguir *(tr)*	distinguish, make out, differentiate **10**
distinguir entre *(tr)*	tell (apart)
distinguirse *(refl)*	excel **10**
distraer *(tr)*	distract **55**
distribuir *(tr)*	distribute **12**
disuadir *(tr)*	dissuade **4**
divagar *(intr)*	ramble on, waffle **7**
divertir *(tr)*	amuse, divert, entertain **22**
divertirse *(refl)*	enjoy oneself **22**
dividir *(tr)*	divide **4**
divisar *(tr)*	make out, sight **2**
divorciar(se) *(tr/refl)*	divorce, get divorced **2**
divulgar *(tr)*	divulge, spread **2**
doblar(se) *(tr/refl)*	double; fold, fold up; bend down, bend over **2**
doler *(tr/intr)*	ache, distress, hurt, pain **20**
domar *(tr)*	tame **2**
domesticar *(tr)*	tame **5**
dominar *(tr)*	master *(a subject)*; overlook **2**
dominarse *(refl)*	control oneself **2**
donar *(tr)*	donate **2**
*dormir(se) *(intr/refl)*	sleep; fall asleep **23**
drogar *(tr)*	dope, drug **7**
drogarse *(refl)*	take drugs
duchar(se) *(tr/refl)*	shower **2**
dudar *(tr)*	doubt **2**
duplicar *(tr)*	double; duplicate **5**

durar *(tr/intr)*	hold out, last	**2**
E **echar** *(tr)*	pour; sprout; cast, toss, throw, throw away	**2**
echar de menos *(tr)*	miss *(somebody)*	
echar la culpa *(tr)*	blame	
echar un vistazo *(intr)*	glance	
echar vapor *(intr)*	steam	
echarse *(refl)*	lie (down)	**2**
echarse atrás *(refl)*	back down	
economizar *(tr)*	economize	**6**
editar *(tr)*	edit	**2**
educar *(tr)*	educate	**5**
efectuar *(tr)*	bring about	**15**
ejecutar *(tr)*	execute, realize; carry out; run *(computing)*	**2**
ejercer *(tr)*	exercise; exert; practice	**9**
ejercitarse *(refl)*	exercise	**2**
elaborar *(tr)*	elaborate, make; work out *(plan)*	**2**
electrificar *(tr)*	electrify	**5**
elegir *(tr)*	choose, elect, pick; vote	**11, 24**
elevar *(tr)*	elevate, heighten	**2**
eliminar *(tr)*	eliminate	**2**
elogiar *(tr)*	praise	**2**
embarcar(se) *(tr/refl)*	board, embark, ship	**5**
embellecer *(tr)*	beautify, embellish	**32**
embestir *(tr)*	assault, charge	**24**
emborracharse *(intr)*	get drunk	**2**
embotellar *(tr)*	bottle	**2**
embromar *(tr)*	tease	**2**
emigrar *(tr)*	emigrate	**2**
emitir *(tr)*	broadcast, emit, issue	**4**
emocionar *(tr)*	excite, move	**2**
empapar *(tr)*	soak, steep	**2**
empapelar *(tr)*	paper	**2**
empaquetar *(tr)*	package	**2**
emparejar *(tr)*	match	**2**
empastar *(tr)*	fill *(a tooth)*	**2**

empatar *(intr)*	tie *(in sport)* **2**
empeorar *(intr)*	get worse, worsen **2**
empezar *(tr/intr)*	begin, get started, start **6, 19**
emplastar *(tr)*	plaster *(medical)* **2**
emplazar *(tr)*	place, site **6**
emplear *(tr)*	employ, use **2**
empollar *(tr)*	incubate, sit on **2**
empotrar *(tr)*	build in **2**
emprender *(tr)*	take on, take up, undertake **3**
empujar *(tr/intr)*	push; prod, shove **2**
emulsionar *(tr)*	emulsify **2**
enajenar *(tr)*	alienate **2**
enamorar(se) de *(tr/refl)*	fall in love with **2**
encadenar *(tr)*	chain up **2**
encajonar *(tr)*	box up **2**
encanecer *(intr)*	go gray **32**
encantar *(tr)*	charm, enchant **2**
encarar *(tr)*	confront **2**
encarcelar *(tr)*	imprison **2**
encargar *(tr)*	commission, order **7**
encauzar *(tr)*	channel **6**
encender(se) *(tr/refl)*	turn on; light, ignite, strike *(match)* **19**
encerrar *(tr)*	confine, enclose, shut in **19**
enclavijar *(tr)*	peg **2**
encoger(se) *(tr/refl)*	flinch, shrink **11**
encogerse de hombros *(refl)*	shrug
encontrar(se) *(tr/refl)*	find; meet, run into **20**
encorvar(se) *(tr/refl)*	bend over, stoop, curve **2**
enderezar(se) *(tr/refl)*	straighten **6**
endosar *(tr)*	endorse **2**
endulzar *(tr)*	sweeten **6**
endurecer(se) *(tr/refl)*	harden **32**
enfadar(se) *(tr/refl)*	anger, annoy; get annoyed **2**
enfermar(se) *(intr/refl)*	fall ill, sick **2**
enfrascar *(tr)*	bottle; get involved **5**
enfrentarse *(refl)*	confront, face up **2**
enfriar *(tr)*	cool down **14**
enfurecer *(tr)*	enrage, madden **32**

VERB INDEX

enganchar *(tr)*	hook; harness (*horse to a cart*) **2**
engañar *(tr)*	bluff, deceive, fool, trick **2**
engordar *(tr/intr)*	fatten **2**
engrasar *(tr)*	grease **2**
engullir *(tr)*	guzzle, swallow **16**
enhebrar *(tr)*	thread **19**
enjabonar *(tr)*	soap **2**
enjaezar *(tr)*	harness **6**
enjuagar *(tr)*	rinse **7**
enjugar *(tr)*	dry, wipe **2, 21**
enlazar *(tr)*	bind, tie **6**
enlazar con *(tr)*	link with
enloquecer *(tr)*	madden **32**
enlucir *(tr)*	plaster **43**
enmarcar *(tr)*	frame **5**
enmendar *(tr)*	amend **19**
enmohecer(se)	get moldy **32**
ennegrecer(se) *(tr/refl)*	blacken **32**
enojar(se) *(tr/refl)*	anger; annoy, get angry **2**
enriquecer *(tr)*	enrich **32**
enrollar *(tr/intr)*	coil, roll open **2**
ensanchar *(tr)*	broaden, enlarge, widen **2**
ensartar *(tr)*	string (*together*), thread **2**
ensayar *(tr)*	rehearse, try **2**
enseñar *(tr/intr)*	show; teach **2**
ensillar *(tr)*	saddle **2**
ensordecer *(tr)*	deafen **32**
ensortijar *(tr)*	curl **2**
ensuciar(se) *(tr/refl)*	dirty, soil **2**
entender *(tr)*	understand **19**
enterrar *(tr)*	bury **19**
entrampar *(tr)*	trap **2**
entrar *(tr/intr)*	enter, get in, go in, go into **2**
entrar en un fichero *(tr)*	access (*a file*)
entrar violentamente *(intr)*	burst in
entreabrir *(tr)*	half open **25**
entregar *(tr)*	deliver, hand in; turn over, yield **7**

entregar(se) *(tr/refl)*	surrender **7**
entregarse a *(refl)*	become addicted **7**
entrenar *(tr)*	train **2**
entrenarse *(refl)*	get fit, train **2**
entretener *(tr)*	entertain **54**
entretenerse *(refl)*	amuse oneself **54**
entrever *(tr)*	glimpse **58**
entrevistar *(tr)*	interview **2**
entristecer *(tr)*	sadden **32**
entusiasmar *(tr)*	enthuse, excite **2**
envasar *(tr)*	package **2**
envejecer *(intr)*	age **32**
envenenar *(tr)*	poison **2**
*enviar *(tr)*	send **14**
enviar por *(tr)*	send for
enviar por correo *(tr)*	mail, post
enviciarse con	become addicted to **2**
envidiar *(tr)*	envy **2**
envilecer *(tr)*	degrade **32**
envolver *(tr)*	wrap up **20**
enyesar *(tr)*	plaster **2**
equilibrar(se) *(tr/refl)*	balance; break even **2**
equipar de *(tr)*	equip, outfit **2**
equiparar *(tr)*	match **2**
equivocar *(tr)*	mistake someone for **5**
equivocarse *(refl)*	be wrong, be mistaken **5**
*erguir(se) *(tr/refl)*	raise; lift; straighten up **35**
erigir *(tr)*	erect; rear **11**
erosionar *(tr)*	erode **2**
*errar *(intr)*	stray; wander; err **36**
esbozar *(tr)*	sketch out **6**
escabullirse *(refl)*	break off, slip away **16**
escalar *(tr)*	climb, scale **2**
escapar(se) *(refl)*	escape, run away **2**
escardar *(tr)*	weed **2**
esclarecer *(intr)*	clear up **32**
esclavizar *(tr)*	enslave **6**
escocer *(tr)*	sting **9, 20**
escoger *(tr)*	choose, select **11**

VERB INDEX

estar asustado	be scared
estar atrasado	be slow (*clock*)
estar ausente	be absent
estar avergonzado	be ashamed
estar bloqueado	be stuck
estar contento	be happy
estar de acuerdo	agree with
estar de luto	mourn, be in mourning
estar descontento	be unhappy
estar desempleado	be unemployed
estar emparentado con	be related to
estar en contra de	be against
estar enfadado	be angry
estar enojado	be annoyed
estar equivocado	be mistaken
estar estreñido	be constipated
estar ilusionado	be looking forward to
estar insatisfecho	be dissatisfied
estar interesado en	be interested in
estar mareado	be dizzy
estar ocupado	be busy
estar parado	be unemployed
estar plagado de	be crawling with
estar pluriempleado	moonlight
estar presente sin intervenir	stand by
estar separado	be separated
estar situado	be situated
estimar *(tr)*	estimate, quote; prize, rate (*evaluate*), value **2**
estirar(se) *(tr/refl)*	stretch; strain; extend; tighten **2**
estorbar *(tr)*	hinder, thwart **2**
estornudar *(intr)*	sneeze **2**
estrangular *(tr)*	strangle, throttle **2**
estrechar(se) *(tr/refl)*	extend, hold out; narrow; tighten **2**
estrellar *(intr)*	crash **2**
estremecerse *(refl)*	quiver, shiver, shudder **32**

estrenar *(tr)*	release (*film*, etc.); open (*show*); wear for the first time **2**
estropear *(tr)*	harm, ruin, spoil **2**
estructurar *(tr)*	structure **2**
estudiar *(tr/intr)*	study **2**
etiquetar *(tr)*	label **2**
evacuar *(tr)*	evacuate **2**
evadir(se) *(tr/refl)*	dodge, evade, run away **2**
evaluar *(tr)*	appraise, evaluate **2, 10**
evitar *(tr)*	avoid **2**
evocar *(tr)*	evoke **5**
evolucionar *(tr)*	evolve **2**
exagerar *(tr)*	exaggerate **2**
examinar *(tr)*	check, examine **2**
exasperar *(tr)*	exasperate **2**
excavar *(tr)*	dig, hollow out **2**
exceder *(tr)*	exceed, surpass, top **3**
exceptuar *(tr)*	except **15**
excitar *(tr)*	excite, work up (*interest, emotion*, etc.) **2**
exclamar *(tr)*	exclaim **2**
excluir *(tr)*	exclude **12**
exculpar *(tr)*	exonerate **2**
exhalar *(tr)*	exhale **2**
exhibir *(tr)*	exhibit **4**
exigir *(tr)*	demand; require **11**
existir *(intr)*	exist **4**
expedir *(tr)*	dispatch, send off **24**
experimentar *(tr)*	experience, feel; experiment **2**
expirar *(tr)*	expire **2**
explicar *(tr)*	explain, give reasons **5**
explorar *(tr)*	explore **2**
explosionar *(intr)*	blow up, explode **2**
explotar *(tr/intr)*	blow up, explode, set off (*explosion*) **2**
exponer *(tr)*	display, expose **47**
exportar *(tr)*	export **2**
expresar *(tr)*	express **2**
exprimir *(tr)*	squeeze (*out*), wring **4**

extender(se) *(tr/efl)*	stretch, extend, spread; expand: lay out **19**
extender la mano	reach out for
extinguir *(tr)*	extinguish **10**
extraer *(tr)*	extract **55**
extraer minerales *(tr)*	mine
extrañar *(tr)*	find strange; miss **2**
extraviarse *(refl)*	stray **14**

F

fabricar *(tr)*	make, manufacture **5**
facilitar *(tr)*	facilitate; provide supply **2**
facturar *(tr)*	bill; check in (*baggage*) **2**
fallar *(intr)*	fail, miss **2**
falsificar *(tr)*	fake **5**
faltar *(intr)*	be missing lack; fail, let down **2**
fascinar *(tr)*	fascinate **2**
fastidiar *(tr)*	get on someone's nerves, tease **2**
fatigar(se) *(tr/refl)*	tire **7**
favorecer *(tr)*	favor **32**
felicitar *(tr)*	congratulate; compliment **2**
fermentar *(tr/intr)*	ferment **2**
festejar *(tr)*	celebrate, fete **2**
fiarse de *(refl)*	trust **14**
fichar *(tr)*	file; index **2**
fichar (la entrada) *(intr)*	clock in
fichar (la salida) *(intr)*	clock out
fijar *(tr)*	fasten, fix, secure **2**
filmar *(tr)*	film, shoot (*film*) **2**
filtrar(se) *(tr/refl)*	filter, seep **2**
financiar *(tr)*	finance **2**
fingir *(tr/intr)*	fake, feign, pretend **11**
firmar *(tr)*	sign **2**
fletar *(tr)*	charter (*plane, boat*) **2**
flirtear *(intr)*	flirt **2**
florecer *(intr)*	bloom, flourish, flower **32**
flotar *(intr)*	float, hover **2**
fluir *(intr)*	flow, stream **12**
fondear *(intr)*	anchor **2**

VERB INDEX

forjar *(tr)*	fashion, form **2**
formar *(tr)*	fashion, form, shape, train, break someone of a habit **2**
fortalecer *(tr)*	strengthen **32**
forzar *(tr)*	compel, force **6, 20**
forzar la entrada *(intr)*	break in **6**
fotocopiar *(tr)*	(photo)copy, duplicate **2**
fotografiar *(tr)*	photograph, shoot **14**
fracasar *(intr)*	fail **2**
fracturar(se) *(tr/intr)*	fracture **2**
franquear *(tr)*	frank **2**
frecuentar *(tr)*	frequent **2**
fregar *(tr)*	scrub, wash up **7, 19**
*freír *(tr)*	fry **39**
frenar *(intr)*	brake **2**
friccionar *(tr)*	rub **2**
frotar *(tr)*	rub **2**
fruncir(se) *(tr/refl)*	wrinkle **9**
frustrar *(tr)*	frustrate **2**
fugarse *(intr)*	flee **7**
fumar *(tr/intr)*	smoke **2**
funcionar *(intr)*	function, work **2**
fundar *(tr)*	found **2**
fundir(se) *(tr/refl)*	blow (*fuse*), fuse, melt **4**
fusionar(se) *(tr/refl)*	fuse; merge **2**

G

ganar *(tr/intr)*	earn; win **2**
gandulear *(intr)*	idle **2**
garantizar *(tr)*	guarantee, secure **6**
garrapatear *(intr)*	scribble **2**
gastar *(tr)*	spend (*money*); use up; wear out **2**
gemir *(intr)*	groan, moan **24**
generar *(tr)*	generate **2**
girar *(tr/intr)*	gyrate, orbit, spin, turn, wheel **2**
gobernar *(tr/intr)*	govern; steer (*ship*) **19**
golpear *(tr)*	hit, knock, strike **2**
gorjear *(intr)*	sing (*birds*), twitter **2**
gotear *(intr)*	drip, trickle **2**

gozar *(tr)*	enjoy **6**
grabar *(tr)*	engrave; record, tape; save (*computing*) **2**
graduarse *(refl)*	graduate, qualify **15**
granizar *(intr)*	hail (stones) **6**
grapar *(tr)*	staple **2**
graznar *(intr)*	croak, squawk **2**
gritar *(tr/intr)*	call out, shout **2**
*gruñir *(intr)*	grunt, growl **17**
guardar *(tr)*	guard, watch (over); keep, store, put away (safely) **2**
guiar *(tr)*	guide, steer **14**
guiñar *(tr)*	wink **2**
gustar *(tr)*	please (used for *like*) **2**

H

*haber *(intr)*	have (auxiliary) **40**
hablar *(tr/intr)*	talk, speak (*language*) **2**
hablar claro *(intr)*	speak out
hablar mal de *(tr)*	speak ill of
*hacer *(tr)*	do; make **41**
hacer abandonar una costumbre *(tr)*	break someone of a habit
hacer aparecer *(tr)*	conjure up
hacer autostop *(intr)*	hitchhike
hacer callar *(tr)*	silence
hacer camping *(intr)*	camp
hacer circular *(tr)*	circulate
hacer cola *(intr)*	get in line, queue
hacer compras *(intr)*	go shopping
hacer constar *(tr)*	minute, take minutes
hacer contrabando *(tr)*	smuggle
hacer daño *(tr)*	harm
hacer desaparecer *(tr)*	conjure (*make disappear*)
hacer eco *(intr)*	echo
hacer el amor *(intr)*	make love
hacer estallar *(tr)*	trigger off
hacer falta *(tr)*	be necessary (*lack*)
hacer frente *(tr)*	confront, cope with
hacer funcionar *(tr)*	make (something) work; run

VERB INDEX

hacer gala de *(tr)*	show off
hacer gimnasia *(intr)*	do gymnastics
hacer girar *(tr)*	wheel, turn
hacer las maletas	pack suitcases
hacer magia *(intr)*	conjure
hacer mal a *(tr)*	damage, hurt
hacer pasar *(tr)*	show in
hacer turnos *(intr)*	take turns
hacer prisionero *(tr)*	take prisoner
hacer proyectos *(intr)*	make plans
hacer punto *(intr)*	knit
hacer que uno pierda el equilibrio	throw off balance
hacer rodar *(tr)*	roll, wheel
hacer trampas *(intr)*	cheat
hacer trasbordo *(intr)*	change (trains); transfer
hacer tropezar *(tr)*	trip up
hacer una huelga *(intr)*	go on strike
hacer una pausa *(tr)*	pause
hacerse *(refl)*	become (*prospects, existence*) **41**
hacerse a la vela	sail
hacerse mayor	grow up
hacer(se) amigos *(tr/refl)*	become friends
hacer(se) borroso *(tr/refl)*	become blurred
halagar *(tr)*	coax, flatter **7**
helar(se) *(tr/refl)*	chill, ice, freeze **19**
hender(se) *(tr/refl)*	split **19**
heredar *(tr/intr)*	inherit, succeed **2**
herir *(tr)*	hurt, injure, wound **22**
herrar *(tr)*	shoe (*horse*) **19**
hervir *(tr/intr)*	boil **22**
hesitar *(intr)*	hesitate **2**
hilar *(tr)*	spin, twine **2**
hinchar *(tr)*	inflate, swell **2**
hipotecar *(tr)*	mortgage **5**
hojear *(tr)*	browse, leaf through **2**
hospedar *(tr)*	accommodate, house, lodge, put up **2**

hospedarse *(refl)*	stay (*as a guest*)	**2**
***huir** *(tr/intr)*	flee; run away	**12**
humedecer *(tr)*	dampen, moisten, wet	**32**
humillar *(tr)*	humiliate	**2**
hundir(se) *(tr/intr/refl)*	sink, subside	**4**
hurgar *(tr)*	poke	**7**
husmear *(tr)*	sniff out	**2**

I	**idealizar** *(tr)*	idealize	**6**
	idear *(tr)*	devise, think out	**2**
	identificar *(tr)*	identify	**5**
	ignorar *(tr)*	ignore	**2**
	igualar *(tr/intr)*	equal, equalize, even out	**2**
	iluminar *(tr)*	illuminate, light (up)	**2**
	ilustrar *(tr)*	illustrate	**2**
	imaginar(se) *(tr/refl)*	imagine; devise, think out	**2**
	imitar *(tr)*	imitate	**2**
	impacientarse *(refl)*	get impatient	**2**
	impedir *(tr)*	hinder, prevent, stop, thwart	**24**
	implicar *(tr)*	involve	**5**
	imponer *(tr)*	impose	**47**
	imponer contribuciones	tax	
	importar *(tr)*	import	**2**
	importar *(intr)*	be important, import, matter	**2**
	importunar *(tr)*	disturb, pester	**2**
	impresionar *(tr/intr)*	impress; strike	**2**
	imprimir *(tr)*	print	**4**
	impulsar *(tr)*	impel	**2**
	incapacitar *(tr)*	incapacitate	**2**
	incendiar(se) *(tr/refl)*	ignite	**2**
	incinerar *(tr)*	cremate, incinerate	**2**
	incitar *(tr)*	urge	**2**
	inclinar(se) *(tr/refl)*	bow, nod; bend, lean, stoop; slope	**2**
	incluir *(tr)*	include	**12**
	incorporar(se) *(tr/refl)*	incorporate; join; sit up (*from lying*), get up (*from reclining position*)	**2**
	indicar *(tr)*	indicate, point (out/to), show	**5**

VERB INDEX

intoxicar *(tr)*	intoxicate, poison **5**
intrigar *(intr)*	plot **7**
introducir *(tr)*	introduce, bring in; insert; enter *(computing)* **31**
introducir poco a poco *(tr)*	phase in
inundar *(tr)*	flood **2**
inventar *(tr)*	invent, make up **2**
invertir *(tr)*	invert, reverse, turn around; invest **22**
investigar *(tr)*	investigate, research **2**
invitar *(tr)*	invite, treat **2**
involucrar *(tr)*	involve **2**
inyectar *(tr)*	inject **2**
ionizar *(tr)*	ionize **6**
***ir** *(intr)*	go **42**
ir a	be going to
ir a buscar	go for, go to fetch
ir a caballo *(intr)*	go on a horse, ride a horse
ir bien *(intr)*	fit; suit
ir de compras *(intr)*	go shopping, shop
ir de excursión a pie *(intr)*	hike
ir de prisa *(intr)*	hurry, rush
ir de tiendas *(intr)*	go shopping, shop
ir en bicicleta *(intr)*	cycle, go on a bike, ride a bike
ir más despacio *(intr)*	slow down
irse *(refl)*	go away, leave **42**
irse volando *(refl)*	fly away
irritar *(tr)*	irritate **2**

J

jabonar *(tr)*	soap **2**
jactarse *(refl)*	boast **2**
jadear *(intr)*	gasp, pant **2**
jubilar(se) *(tr/refl)*	retire **2**
***jugar** *(intr)*	play; gamble **21**
jugar el papel de *(intr)*	act out, play a role
juntar(se) *(tr/refl)*	couple, join, pool (resources); assemble, unite **2**
jurar *(tr/intr)*	swear **2**
justificar *(tr)*	justify **5**

juzgar *(tr)*	judge, prosecute, try	**7**
juzgar mal *(tr)*	misjudge	

_L_

labrar *(tr)*	cultivate, farm, till	**2**
ladear *(tr)*	skirt around; incline	**2**
ladrar *(intr)*	bark	**2**
lamentar *(tr/intr)*	be sorry, lament, regret	**2**
lamer *(tr)*	lick	**4**
languidecer *(intr)*	languish, pine (away)	**32**
lanzar *(tr)*	bowl, cast, launch, throw	**6**
largar(se) de *(tr/refl)*	clear off, clear out,	
	get out of way of, go away	**7**
lastimar *(tr)*	damage, hurt	**2**
latir *(intr)*	beat (*heart*)	**4**
lavar(se) *(tr/refl)*	wash	**2**
*leer *(tr/intr)*	read	**13**
leer en voz alta *(tr)*	read aloud	
legalizar *(tr)*	legalize	**6**
legar *(tr)*	bequeath, leave	**7**
legitimar *(tr)*	legalize	**2**
levantar *(tr)*	hoist, lift, raise; erect, rear	**2**
levantar los ojos	look up	
levantarse *(refl)*	get up, stand up	**2**
liar *(tr)*	bind, bond, tie	**14**
libertar *(tr)*	free, set free	**2**
librar(se) de *(tr/refl)*	rid, rid oneself of	**2**
licenciar *(tr)*	license	**2**
licitar *(tr)*	bid	**2**
lijar *(tr)*	sandpaper	**2**
limar *(tr)*	file down	**2**
limitar *(tr)*	limit	**2**
limpiar *(tr)*	clean, polish; tidy up, wipe	**2**
lindar *(tr)*	border	**2**
liquidar *(tr)*	liquidate; pay off, sell cheaply	**2**
lisonjear *(tr)*	flatter	**2**
llamar *(tr)*	call, name, summon, term;	
	send for	**2**
llamar a *(intr)*	call to, hail	
llamar a filas *(tr)*	call up	

llamar con señas *(tr)*	beckon
llamar por teléfono *(tr)*	call, ring (up), (tele)phone
llamear *(intr)*	flare **2**
llegar *(intr)*	arrive; come round (*date*, etc.), reach **7**
llegar tarde	be late
llenar *(tr)*	cram, fill, pack, stuff **2**
llevar *(tr)*	bear, carry; take, transfer; convey; drive someone; have on, wear **2**
llevar a cabo *(tr)*	accomplish, carry out, implement
llevar la batuta *(intr)*	conduct (*orchestra*); be in control
llevar la delantera *(intr)*	lead
llevarse *(refl)*	take out/away (*including food*); get away with; carry off, remove **2**
lleverse bien con *(tr)*	get along with, get on well
llorar *(intr)*	cry, mourn, weep **2**
llover *(intr)*	rain **20**
lloviznar *(intr)*	drizzle **2**
lograr *(tr/intr)*	achieve **2**
lubricar *(tr)*	lubricate **5**
lubrificar *(tr)*	lubricate, oil **5**
luchar *(tr/intr)*	fight, struggle, wrestle **2**
***lucir(se)** *(tr/intr/refl)*	shine; excel; show off **43**

M

machacar *(tr)*	mash, pound **5**
madurar *(tr/intr)*	ripen **2**
magnetizar *(tr)*	magnetize **6**
maldecir *(tr)*	curse, damn **28**
malear(se) *(tr/refl)*	sour **2**
malgastar *(tr)*	waste **2**
malinterpretar *(tr)*	misinterpret **2**
malparir *(intr)*	miscarry **4**
maltratar *(tr)*	abuse, maltreat, mistreat **2**
malversar *(tr)*	embezzle **2**
mamar *(tr)*	suckle **2**
manar *(intr)*	flow, well up **2**
manchar(se) *(tr/refl)*	soil, spot, stain **2**

VERB INDEX

mandar *(tr)*	command, lead; order, tell; send **2**
mandar por correo *(tr)*	mail, post
manejar *(tr)*	manage; operate (*machine*); drive, steer **2**
manifestar *(tr)*	manifest; declare, state **19**
manosear *(tr)*	handle **2**
mantener *(tr)*	keep; maintain, provide for, support **54**
mantenerse alejado *(refl)*	keep away
mantener(se) bien *(tr/refl)*	stand firm, steady
maquillar *(tr)*	apply makeup **2**
marcar *(tr)*	dial; mark; score **5**
marchar *(intr)*	march; function work **2**
marcharse *(intr)*	go away, leave **2**
marchitar(se) *(tr/intr/refl)*	wither, wilt **2**
marearse *(refl)*	get sick/dizzy **2**
marginarse *(refl)*	drop out (*of society*) **2**
martillar *(tr)*	hammer **2**
masacrar *(tr)*	massacre **2**
mascar *(tr)*	chew **5**
masticar *(tr)*	chew **5**
matar *(tr)*	kill, murder, slaughter **2**
matar con arma de fuego *(tr)*	shoot (*dead*)
matricular(se) *(tr/refl)*	enroll in **2**
maullar *(intr)*	meow **2**
mecer(se) *(tr/refl)*	rock **9**
medir *(tr/intr)*	measure **24**
medir el tiempo	time
meditar *(intr)*	meditate **2**
mejorar(se) *(tr/refl)*	improve **2**
mencionar *(tr/intr)*	mention, refer to **2**
mendigar *(tr)*	beg (*as a beggar*) **7**
menear(se) *(tr/refl)*	bustle, rush about; stir; wag **2**
menospreciar *(tr)*	despise, disparage **2**
mentir *(intr)*	lie **22**
mercadear *(tr)*	market **2**
merecer *(tr)*	deserve **32**

merendar en el campo *(intr)* — picnic **19**
meter *(tr)* — put in, stock **3**
mezclar *(tr/intr)* — blend, jumble up, mix **2**
migrar *(intr)* — migrate **2**
mimar *(tr)* — spoil (*child*) **2**
mirar *(tr/intr)* — gaze, look (at), watch, view **2**
  mirar boquiabierto *(tr)* — gape at
  mirar fijamente *(tr)* — stare
  mirar furtivamente *(tr)* — peep
  mirar rápidamente *(tr)* — peep
modelar *(tr)* — model **2**
moderar la marcha *(intr)* — slow down, draw in **2**
modernizar *(tr)* — modernize, update **6**
modificar *(tr)* — modify, vary **5**
mojar *(tr)* — dampen, dip, moisten, soak, wet **2**
moldear *(tr)* — mold, shape **2**
moler *(tr)* — grind, mill **20**
molestar *(tr)* — bother, disturb, molest, pester **2**
molestar(se) *(tr/refl)* — trouble; get angry **2**
mondar *(tr)* — peel **2**
monopolizar *(tr)* — monopolize **6**
montar *(tr)* — assemble, erect; mount **2**
  montar *(en) (tr/intr)* — ride
  montar a caballo *(intr)* — go horse riding
morder *(tr)* — bite **20**
mordiscar *(tr/intr)* — nibble **5**
morir *(intr)* — die **23**
  morir de hambre *(intr)* — starve (*to death*)
mortificar *(tr)* — spite **5**
mostrar *(tr)* — show **20**
motivar *(tr)* — motivate **2**
mover(se) *(tr/refl)* — move; wag **20**
mudar(se) *(tr/refl)* — change; molt; move house **2**
muestrear *(tr)* — sample **2**
multar *(tr)* — fine **2**
multiplicar(se) *(tr/refl)* — multiply **5**
murmullar *(tr/intr)* — murmur **2**

odiar *(tr)*	hate **2**
ofender *(tr)*	offend **19**
ofrecer *(tr)*	offer; bid **32**
***oír** *(tr/intr)*	hear; listen; pay attention **44**
***oler** *(tr/intr)*	smell; sniff **45**
olfatear *(tr)*	sniff **2**
olvidar *(tr/intr)*	forget, leave behind, overlook **2**
omitir *(tr)*	leave out, omit **4**
ondular *(tr/intr)*	wave **2**
operar *(tr/intr)*	operate **2**
opinar *(tr/intr)*	have an opinion, have the opinion that, think of **2**
oponer(se) a *(tr/intr)*	oppose, stand out against **47**
optar por *(tr)*	decide on, opt for **2**
orar *(intr)*	pray **2**
orbitar *(tr/intr)*	orbit **2**
ordenar *(tr)*	command, order, put in order, sort **2**
ordeñar *(tr)*	milk **2**
organizar *(tr)*	organize **6**
orinar *(intr)*	urinate **2**
osar *(intr)*	dare **2**
oscilar (entre) *(intr)*	range (*between*); oscillate, sway, swing **2**
oscurecer *(intr)*	darken; grow dark **32**
ostentar *(tr)*	show off; boast; hold a post **2**
otorgar *(tr)*	award (*prize*, etc.); confer, grant **7**
oxidar(se) *(tr/refl)*	oxidize, rust **2**

P

pacer *(tr/intr)*	graze **32**
padecer *(tr/intr)*	suffer **32**
padecer hambre *(intr)*	starve
***pagar** *(tr/intr)*	pay **7**
pagar y marcharse	check out
palear *(tr)*	paddle (*boat*); shovel **2**
palidecer *(intr)*	turn pale **32**
palpar *(tr)*	feel, touch **2**
palpitar *(intr)*	beat, palpitate, pound **2**

VERB INDEX

peinar *(tr)*	comb **2**
pelar *(tr)*	peel, cut hair **2**
pelearse *(refl)*	argue, fight, quarrel **2**
pellizcar *(tr)*	pinch **5**
pender *(intr)*	hang **3**
penetrar *(tr)*	penetrate; see through **2**
***pensar** *(tr/intr)*	think; intend **19**
pensar en *(tr)*	think of
pensionar *(tr)*	pension **2**
percibir *(tr)*	discern, perceive, sense **4**
perder *(tr/intr)*	lose **19**
perder el conocimiento *(intr)*	faint, pass out
perder el tiempo *(intr)*	loiter, lose time
perder la paciencia *(intr)*	lose one's temper
perderse *(refl)*	get lost, stray **19**
perdonar *(tr)*	forgive, let off, pardon, spare (*life*) **2**
perdurar *(intr)*	remain unchanged **2**
perecer *(intr)*	perish **32**
perfeccionar(se) *(tr/refl)*	improve, perfect **2**
perfilar *(tr)*	outline **2**
perforar *(tr)*	perforate; drill; sink (*well*) **2**
perfumar *(tr)*	perfume, scent **2**
perjudicar *(tr)*	damage, harm **5**
permanecer *(intr)*	remain, stay **32**
permitir *(tr)*	allow, let, permit **4**
pernoctar *(intr)*	spend the night somewhere **2**
perpetuar *(tr)*	perpetuate **15**
perseguir *(tr/intr)*	chase, hound, pursue **10, 24**
persistir *(intr)*	keep on, persist **4**
persuadir *(tr)*	persuade **4**
pertenecer *(intr)*	belong **32**
perturbar *(tr)*	disturb **2**
pesar *(tr/intr)*	weigh **2**
pescar *(tr)*	fish **5**
pestañear *(intr)*	blink **2**
picar *(tr)*	prick, sting, itch; mince (*food*); bite (*insect*) **5**
picotear *(tr/intr)*	peck **2**

VERB INDEX

ponerse en camino	set off, start, start out
ponerse enfermo	become ill
poner(se) moreno *(tr/refl)*	tan
ponerse nervioso	get worked up
portarse *(refl)*	behave **2**
poseer *(tr)*	own, possess, have **13**
posponer *(tr)*	postpone **47**
potenciar *(tr)*	potentiate **2**
practicar *(tr/intr)*	drill, practice **5**
precipitar(se) *(tr/refl)*	precipitate, rush, hasten **2**
precisar *(tr)*	pin (oneself) down **2**
predecir *(tr)*	predict **34**
predicar *(tr/intr)*	preach **5**
preferir *(tr)*	prefer **22**
preguntar *(tr)*	ask, inquire, question **2**
preguntar por	ask for/after (*a person*)
preguntarse *(refl)*	ask oneself, wonder **2**
prender *(tr)*	capture, take **3**
prender con un alfiler *(tr)*	pin
preocupar(se) *(refl)*	worry **2**
preparar(se) *(tr/refl)*	get ready, prepare **2**
prescindir de *(tr)*	dispense with, do without **4**
presenciar *(tr)*	witness **2**
presentar *(tr)*	display, present, send in; show (e.g., *ticket*) **2**
presentarse a *(refl)*	apply (*for a job*); go in for, show up
preservar *(tr)*	preserve **2**
presidir *(tr/intr)*	chair, preside **4**
presionar *(tr)*	depress, press (*button*, etc.), push down **2**
prestar *(tr)*	lend **2**
prestar atención *(intr)*	pay attention
presupuestar *(tr)*	budget **2**
pretender *(tr)*	pretend; seek to **3**
prevenir *(tr)*	prevent, warn **57**
prever *(tr)*	forecast, foresee **58**
privar de *(tr)*	deprive, do out of **2**
privar de comida *(tr)*	starve

VERB INDEX

pulverizar(se) *(tr/refl)*	pulverize	**6**
purificar *(tr)*	purify, refine	**5**

Q

quebrar(se) *(tr/refl)*	break, smash	**19**
quedar *(intr)*	remain, stay	**2**
quedar en pie *(intr)*	remain standing, stand	
quedar en *(tr)*	decide on	
quedar sin *(tr)*	run out of	
quedar(se) *(refl)*	stay, remain, stay behind	**2**
quedarse atrás	drop behind	
quedarse dormido *(intr)*	fall asleep, nod off	
quejar(se) *(intr/refl)*	complain, groan, grumble, moan	**2**
*querer *(tr)*	want; wish; love	**48**
querer *(+ infinitive)*	want to do something	
querer decir *(tr)*	mean	
quitar(se) *(tr/refl)*	take off; clear away; withdraw; remove, take away	**2**
quitar el polvo *(tr)*	dust	

R

racionar *(tr)*	ration	**2**
radiografiar *(tr)*	X-ray	**14**
raer *(tr)*	scrape	**30**
rajar(se) *(tr/refl)*	crack, split; expel	**2**
rallar *(tr)*	grate	**2**
raptar *(tr)*	kidnap	**2**
rascar(se) *(tr/refl)*	scratch	**5**
rasgar(se) *(tr/refl)*	tear	**7**
rasguñar *(tr/intr)*	scratch	**2**
raspar *(tr)*	scrape	**2**
rastrear *(tr)*	track, trail	**2**
rastrillar *(tr)*	rake	**2**
ratificar *(tr)*	endorse, ratify	**5**
rayar *(tr)*	rule *(paper)*	**2**
razonar *(intr)*	reason	**2**
reaccionar *(tr)*	react	**2**
realizar *(tr)*	carry out, perform; fulfill, make real, realize; achieve, complete	**6**

VERB INDEX

reducir la velocidad *(tr/intr)*	slow down
reducir progresivamente *(tr)*	phase out
reembolsar *(tr)*	refund, reimburse **2**
reemplazar *(tr)*	replace **6**
referirse a *(refl)*	refer to **22**
refinar *(tr)*	refine **2**
reflejar *(tr)*	reflect **2**
reflexionar *(intr)*	reflect, think over **2**
reforzar *(tr)*	reinforce, strengthen **6, 20**
refrenar *(tr)*	restrain, stem **2**
refrescar(se) *(tr/refl)*	freshen, refresh **5**
refrigerar *(tr)*	refrigerate **2**
refunfuñar *(intr)*	grumble **2**
refutar *(tr)*	refute **2**
regalar *(tr)*	give away *(as a present)* **2**
regañar *(tr)*	nag, scold **2**
regar *(tr)*	irrigate, spray, water *(plants)* **7, 19**
regatear *(intr)*	bargain, haggle **2**
regentar *(tr)*	boss about **2**
regir *(tr)*	govern, rule **11, 24**
registrar *(tr)*	register, record, enroll; look through, scan **2**
registrarse *(refl)*	register *(in a hotel)*
reglamentar *(intr)*	make regulations, regulate **2**
regocijar(se) *(tr/refl)*	rejoice **2**
regresar *(intr)*	come/go home/back, get back, return **2**
regular *(tr)*	regulate **2**
regularizar *(tr)*	standardize **6**
rehacer *(tr)*	redo; remake **41**
rehusar *(intr)*	refuse **2**
reinar *(intr)*	reigns, rule **2**
reintegrar *(tr)*	refund **2**
reiterar *(tr)*	reiterate **2**
***reír(se)** *(refl)*	laugh **49**
relacionar *(tr)*	relate **2**
relajar *(tr/intr)*	relax **2**
relampaguear *(intr)*	flash (lightning) **2**

resistir *(intr)*	resist, stand up to; endure, hold out **4**
resollar *(intr)*	pant **2**
resolver *(tr)*	resolve, solve, figure/work out *(solution)* **20**
resolver(se) a *(tr/refl)*	make up one's mind, resolve (to) **20**
resonar *(intr)*	blare, resound, sound **20**
respaldar *(tr)*	support **2**
respetar *(tr)*	respect **2**
respirar *(intr)*	breathe **2**
respirar con dificultad *(intr)*	gasp
responder *(tr)*	reply **3**
responder de *(tr)*	account for
restar *(tr)*	subtract **2**
restaurar *(tr)*	restore **2**
restregar *(tr)*	rub, scrub **7**
restringir *(tr)*	limit, restrict **11**
resucitar *(tr/intr)*	revive **2**
resultar *(intr)*	result, turn out, work out **2**
resumir *(tr)*	summarize, sum up **4**
retar *(tr)*	challenge **2**
retardar *(tr)*	delay, slow down **2**
retener *(tr)*	hold back, keep back, retain **54**
retirar(se) *(tr/refl)*	retire; cancel; take out, withdraw *(money from bank*, etc.) **2**
retorcer(se) *(tr/refl)*	twist **9**
retransmitir *(tr)*	relay **4**
retrasar *(tr)*	delay **2**
retroceder *(intr)*	stand back, turn back **3**
retumbar *(intr)*	resound, rumble **2**
reunir(se) *(tr/refl)*	join, reunite, rejoin; collect, gather, meet **15**
revelar *(tr)*	disclose, reveal, show **2**
reventar *(intr)*	burst, explode **19**
revestir *(tr)*	coat, cover **24**
revestir de acero *(tr)*	cover with steel
revestir de hormigón *(tr)*	cover with concrete
revisar *(tr)*	check, check over, revise **2**

revisar cuentas	audit
revolotear *(intr)*	fly about, wheel **2**
revolver *(intr)*	turn around **20**
rezar *(intr)*	pray **6**
ridiculizar *(tr)*	ridicule **6**
rizar *(tr)*	curl **6**
robar *(tr)*	burglarize/burgle, rob, steal **2**
rociar *(tr)*	spatter, sprinkle **14**
rodar *(intr)*	bowl; roll, wheel; shoot (*film*) **20**
rodear *(tr)*	circle, close in, encircle, skirt, surround **2**
roer *(tr)*	gnaw **30**
rogar *(tr)*	beg, plead, pray, request **7, 20**
*romper(se) *(tr/refl)*	break **50**
roncar *(intr)*	snore **5**
ronronear *(intr)*	purr **2**
rozar *(tr)*	brush against **6**
ruborizarse *(refl)*	blush **6**
rugir *(intr)*	roar **11**

S

*saber *(tr/intr)*	know; know how to; learn **51**
saborear *(tr)*	savor **2**
*sacar *(tr)*	take out, get out, withdraw; stick out; draw **5**
sacar con cuchara *(tr)*	scoop
sacar de quicio *(tr)*	irritate, madden
sacar ganancia (de) *(intr)*	benefit, profit (from)
sacar una foto *(tr)*	take a photograph
saciar *(tr)*	quench **2**
sacrificar *(tr)*	sacrifice **5**
sacudir(se) *(tr/refl)*	rock, shake **4**
salar *(tr)*	salt **2**
saldar *(tr)*	pay off **2**
*salir *(intr)*	get/go/come out; exit, leave, depart; branch off; rise (*sun, moon*) **52**
salir a escena *(intr)*	come on (stage)
salir bien *(intr)*	come out well, succeed
salir mal *(intr)*	turn out badly

salir como un huracán	storm out
salir del huevo *(intr)*	hatch out
salir violentamente *(intr)*	burst out
salpicar *(tr)*	scatter, spatter, splash, sprinkle **5**
saltar *(intr)*	jump, leap, spring **2**
saludar *(tr)*	greet **2**
salvar *(tr)*	salvage, save **2**
sanar *(tr/intr)*	heal **2**
sangrar *(intr)*	bleed **2**
satisfacer *(tr)*	satisfy **41**
sazonar *(tr)*	season **2**
secar(se) *(tr/refl)*	wipe, dry, dry out **5**
secuestrar *(tr)*	hijack, kidnap **2**
seducir *(tr)*	lure, seduce **31**
segar *(tr)*	mow, reap **7**
seguir *(tr/intr)*	continue, go on; keep (on) . . . ing; come after, follow **10, 24**
seguir fiel a *(intr)*	stick to
seleccionar *(tr)*	choose, pick, select **2**
sellar *(tr)*	seal **2**
sembrar *(tr)*	plant, sow **19**
señalar *(tr)*	indicate, point (out/to); sign, signal **2**
sentar(se) *(tr/refl)*	sit, seat (someone else); suit **19**
sentarse a la mesa *(refl)*	sit at table
sentenciar *(tr)*	sentence **2**
*sentir *(tr/intr)*	feel, sense; be sorry, regret **22**
separar(se) de *(tr/refl)*	break off, separate, spread out **2**
sepultar *(tr)*	bury **2**
*ser *(intr)*	be **53**
ser cuestión de *(intr)*	be a matter of
ser diferente de	be different from
ser escritor *(intr)*	be a writer (*career*)
ser una estrella *(intr)*	star
ser miembro de	be a member of
ser necesario	be necessary

ser operado	have an operation
ser paciente	be patient
ser permitido	be allowed
ser responsable de	be liable for, be responsible for
ser socio de	be a member of
ser valedero	be valid
serrar *(tr)*	saw **19**
servir *(tr)*	serve **24**
servir a alguien *(tr)*	wait on someone
servir para *(intr)*	to be useful for
servirse *(refl)*	help oneself **24**
servirse de *(refl)*	make use of
sesgar *(tr)*	put skew, slant **7**
significar *(tr)*	denote, mean, signify **5**
silbar *(intr)*	whistle; hiss **2**
simular *(tr)*	pretend **2**
sintetizar *(tr)*	synthesize **6**
sintonizar *(intr)*	tune in **6**
sisar *(tr)*	steal, swipe **2**
sisear *(intr)*	hiss **2**
sitiar *(tr)*	besiege **2**
situar *(tr)*	place, site, situate **15**
sobornar *(tr)*	bribe **2**
sobrepasar *(tr)*	surpass **2**
sobresalir *(intr)*	jut out, overhang; stand out; bulge **52**
sobresaltar(se) *(tr/refl)*	alarm, frighten, shock, start, startle **2**
sobrevivir *(intr)*	survive **4**
sofocar(se) *(tr/refl)*	choke, suffocate **5**
soldar(se) *(tr/refl)*	weld **20**
soler *(tr)*	be accustomed to **20**
solicitar *(tr)*	beg for, request **2**
solidificar(se) *(tr/refl)*	solidify **5**
sollozar *(intr)*	sob **6**
soltar *(tr)*	let go, release; cast off *(boat)*; loosen **20**
solucionar *(tr)*	solve **2**
sombrear *(tr)*	shade **2**

someter(se) *(tr/refl)*	submit, subject; yield **3**
sonar *(tr/intr)*	sound **20**
soñar *(tr/intr)*	dream **20**
soñar despierto *(intr)*	daydream
sonreír *(intr)*	smile **49**
sonrojarse *(refl)*	blush **2**
soplar *(intr)*	blow **2**
soportar *(tr)*	bear, endure, stand, support **2**
sorber *(tr)*	sip **3**
sorprender *(tr)*	catch out, surprise **3**
sosegar *(tr)*	calm **7, 19**
sospechar *(tr)*	suspect **2**
sostener *(tr)*	hold up, support, sustain **54**
subir *(intr)*	climb, get on, increase (*prices*), go up; come in (*tide*), rise (e.g., *slope*) **4**
subir (a) *(tr)*	increase, lift, raise; board, climb **4**
sublevarse *(refl)*	rebel **2**
subrayar *(tr)*	emphasize, highlight, stress, underline **2**
subsidiar *(tr)*	subsidize **2**
subvencionar *(tr)*	subsidize **2**
suceder *(intr)*	happen, occur; follow, succeed **3**
sudar *(intr)*	sweat **2**
sufrir *(tr/intr)*	suffer, undergo **4**
sugerir *(tr)*	suggest **22**
sujetar *(tr)*	attach, fasten, fix; clamp, hold down **2**
sujetar con un peso *(tr)*	weigh down
sumar *(tr/intr)*	add, amount, number **2**
sumergir(se) *(tr/refl/intr)*	immerse, plunge, submerge **11**
suministrar *(tr)*	furnish, provide, supply **2**
superar *(tr)*	overcome, surpass **2**
supervisar *(tr)*	supervise **2**
suplicar *(tr)*	beg, pray **5**
suplir *(intr)*	stand in for, substitute **4**
suponer *(tr)*	suppose **47**

VERB INDEX

suprimir *(tr)*	abolish, excise, suppress	**4**
surgir *(intr)*	arise (e.g., *problem*)	**11**
surtir *(tr)*	stock, supply	**4**
suscribir *(intr)*	subscribe	**37**
suspender *(tr)*	suspend, call off; give a failing grade	**3**
suspirar *(intr)*	sigh	**2**
suspirar por *(intr)*	pine for	
sustituir *(tr)*	change, replace, substitute	**12**
sustraer *(tr)*	subtract	**55**
susurrar *(intr)*	whisper	**2**

T

tachar *(tr)*	cross out, delete, erase	**2**
tajar *(tr)*	chop, cut, hack, slice	**2**
taladrar *(tr)*	drill	**2**
tallar *(tr)*	hew	**2**
tambalear(se) *(intr/refl)*	stagger, totter	**2**
tamborilear *(intr)*	drum/patter	**2**
tamizar *(tr)*	screen, sieve, sift	**6**
tañer *(tr)*	pluck, play (*instrument*)	**17**
tapar *(tr)*	block, plug	**2**
taponar *(tr)*	cork	**2**
tardar *(intr)*	delay, linger	**2**
tartamudear *(intr)*	stammer, stutter	**2**
tasar *(tr)*	appraise, price	**2**
techar *(tr)*	put a roof on	**2**
tejer *(tr/intr)*	spin (*wool*), weave	**3**
telefonear *(tr)*	call, (tele)phone	**2**
temblar *(intr)*	quiver, shiver, tremble	**19**
temer *(tr)*	dread, fear	**3**
templar *(tr)*	moderate, temper	**2**
tender(se) *(tr/refl)*	lie, spread, stretch out	**19**
tender a *(intr)*	tend, be likely to	
tender una embuscada *(intr)*	ambush	
***tener** *(tr)*	have; hold	**54**
tener aversión a *(tr)*	dislike	
tener cariño a *(tr)*	have affection for	
tener cuidado *(intr)*	look out, take care	